HOT Springs
& Hot Pools
of the Northwest

HOT Springs & Hot Pools of the Northwest

Jayson Loam's Original Guide

Marjorie Gersh-Young

AQUA THERMAL ACCESS

*Hot Springs and Hot Pools of the Northwest:
Jayson Loam's Original Guide*

Copyright 2003 by Marjorie Gersh-Young

Design, layout, and production
by Marjorie Gersh-Young

Front Cover - Weir Creek, ID / Chris Andrews
Back Cover - Sloquet Creek Hot Springs, CD
/ Phil Wilcox

ISBN 1-890880-04-3

Manufactured in the United States

Published by: **Aqua Thermal Access**
55 Azalea Lane
Santa Cruz, CA 95060
831 426-2956
email: hsprings@ix.netcom.com
web page: www.hotpools.com

Grateful acknowledgements to:

All of the regional contributors who always went above and beyond their assignment to make this book interesting and accurate. All of you who have written in with updates and information. Staff members at state parks, national forests, national parks, and hot springs resorts for their cooperation and encouragement. A special thanks to Jane Leche, Public Affairs Specialist for the US Forest Service for her help with the Caring For the Outdoors section. Bill Gumbiner, my heartfelt thanks for editing the manuscript, a very tedious job. My husband Henry, for his support and his "eagle eye." My friend Debbie, for her patience and help whenever asked for.

Please Note: It is not possible to include all of the dangers encountered in getting to and making use of the hot springs described in this book. It is up to you, the reader, to use common sense and learn as much as you can about the risks involved and the safety measures needed.

TABLE OF CONTENTS

INTRODUCTION

By Marjorie Gersh-Young

The caretaker at Burgdorf Hot Springs loves to create new art works out of wood that he finds around the property. Here I am with my husband Henry posing under one of his creations on our trip to update this new edition.

This book was written with the premise that there is nothing more enjoyable than to soak in a hot spring in ideal conditions. To me this means a beautiful pool with water at 104° cascading in over the rocks out in the middle of the forest at the end of a moderate hike. While definitions of the perfect pool may differ, there does seem to be some standard information that everyone wants to know in order to make an informed choice.

Our hot springs research program started with an analysis of the 1,600 springs listed in the NOAA springs list published by the National Oceanic and Atmospheric Administration. Only seven percent of the listed springs were on public land, accessible without charge, and another fifteen percent were private, commercial enterprises open to the public. Nearly one-third of the locations had temperatures below 90°, so we eliminated them as simply not hot enough. The remaining two-thirds required individual investigation, usually involving personal inspection, which reduced the NOAA list to a usable twenty-two percent. The unusable seventy-eight percent were often old resorts that had burned down, seeps too small to get into, functioning as cattle troughs, or on posted, private land, making them not usable by the public (NUBP).

As many of you may know, Jayson Loam was the original creator of these hot spring books over twenty years ago. At that time, he did the initial field work and made many decisions as to what information should be included or excluded. Over the years we have refined the format, but without going into an analysis of the chemicals in the water, have maintained the basic premise that soaking in geothermal water does feel good. We have continued to designate hot water as anything above 90° and to include hot wells, treating them the same as hot springs. (Occasionally, I will include a spring at a lower temperature due to its natural beauty or location.) Rental tub locations, which have now become an integral part of many people's lives, are also included. And, as a special service and option for many of our readers, there is now a listing of nudist/naturist resorts and parks in those states where there are springs listed that welcome visitors with advance reservations. One thing we do not do is send people onto private property where they can get arrested or shot.

This edition retains these basic criteria while expanding the descriptions, providing more detailed directions with GPS coordinates, and adding a bit of history whenever possible. I feel sure that the blending of our styles and interests will ensure you, the user, continued enjoyment from the book.

Jayson Loam
1918-1994

There is no way I can publish a new edition without including a special mention of Jayson. Without his passion for doing what he truly loved to do most, searching out hot springs and writing about them, this book would not exist and many of us would never have been introduced to the pleasures of hot water. He was truly "King of the Hot Springs."

REGIONAL CONTRIBUTORS

CHRIS ANDREWS, who lives and works in Idaho seems to like nothing better than to hop in his truck and travel to hot springs all over the west. He takes wonderful photographs and doesn't mind how far he has to hike to find a spring he hasn't visited. He's also a whiz with a map and a GPS and many of the accurate detailed directions are due to his diligence.

PHIL WILCOX, also known as "The Solar Man", is mostly retired and lives comfortably in his solar home in Northern California. He loves to travel, usually in his 4WD, solar equipped camper van. He has visited all fifty States and some twenty-four other countries but loves the beauty of our Northwest the best, from California to Alaska. He may be reached at PO Box 1460, Lower Lake, Ca. 95457 or email to thesolarman@yahoo.com. GPS: N 38.5354 W. 122.3136.

SKIP HILL, intrepid hot spring adventurer, writer and publisher of the *Hot Springs Gazette*, has been more than kind in offering advice, directions, photos, and bits of information to make the information in this book more accurate and allowing me to add some of his "finds."

To subscribe to this off-beat and delightful journal see the ad in the back of this book or proceed to his website: www.hotspringsgazette.com.

CAMILLA VAN SICKLE AND BILL PENNINGTON have fulfilled their dreams after many years of traveling to track down hundreds of remote hot springs and natural locations. Seven years ago, they opened El Dorado Hot Spring midway between Phoenix, Arizona and the California border. They offer natural hot mineral water, massage, lodging, camping, a stone labyrinth, contemplative space, and smoke and alcohol free common areas in a clean, simple desert oasis for your soaking and relaxation pleasure. During the frequent vacations these inveterate explorers take, they investigate 'new' hot springs and offer updates for this publication on existing ones. POB 10, Tonopah, Arizona 85354. www.HotSpring@El-Dorado.com.

DEBBIE JOHNSON, a wonderful traveling companion, discovered hot springs through her interest in travel and collecting varied wild mushrooms. Fungi and hot springs are found in beautiful, remote areas. A soak after a day's hiking, bending and picking is certainly a welcome pleasure. Debbie and her husband Fred enjoy trips to investigate new hot springs and revisit old favorites.

And a very special thanks to:

Oscar Voss
The Idaho Dippers—Stephanie and Chuck Ensign
Nick Hertelendy
Tom Smith
And all of the other contributors who sent information, pictures, and comments.

HUNTING FOR HOT WATER:
Where it Comes From

The cataclysmic folding and faulting of the earth's crust over millions of years, combined with just the right amount of underground water and earth core magma, has produced a hot surface geothermal flow that often goes on for centuries.

As volcanic activity dies down, igneous rocks which have solidified from hot liquids such as magma are formed in pockets deep in the earth below the remains of the volcano. The magma produces heat which is conducted through a layer of solid rock into the porous level where new water, or water which has never before been on the surface, is believed to be formed from available molecules. Fissures are formed in the solid rock layer above the porous layer and steam and hot water escape producing hot springs, geysers, and fumaroles. A hot spring is considered to be a natural flow of water from the ground at a single point. It is called a seep if it does not have enough flow to create a current. Springs may come up on dry land or in the beds of streams, ponds, and lakes.

Natural geothermal areas lie in the earthquake and volcano belts along the earth's crustal plates. In many areas, due to the earth shifting and moving, the hot magma has worked its way closer to the earth's surface. Surface water (water from rain, for instance) soaks into the earth through cracks and crevices down to the area where the hot magma again provides the heat source for the water. If there are no fissures or cracks for the water to use to come to the surface, wells can be drilled, for example. Each of the resorts in Desert Hot Springs, California has its own well.

Water temperatures vary greatly. When the water is at least fourteen degrees hotter than the average temperature of the air it is considered to be thermal water (or a hot springs). This definition means that there is a very wide range of what is considered thermal water as the air temperature in Iceland is certainly different from that of a California desert. The overall temperature of the water can range up to the boiling point. Geothermal resources in Italy, New Zealand, California, and Iceland have been used for a number of years to heat municipal and private buildings, and even whole towns. In Iceland, the early Norse carried hot water to their homes through wooden pipes.

As the water travels up through varying layers of the earth, it accumulates different properties. These are classified as alkaline, saline, chalybeate or iron, sulfurous, acidulous, and arsenical. At least as far back as the time of the Greeks and the Romans, medicinal cures were attributed to the different chemicals and certain springs were alleged to cure certain ailments from venereal diseases to stomach and urinary tract weaknesses. The waters were administered in a combination of drinking and soaking.

Of the thousands of hot springs found in the United States, most are found in the Western mountains.

A Bit of History

Long before the "white man" arrived to "discover" hot springs, the Native Americans believed that the Great Spirit resided in the center of the earth and that "Big Medicine" fountains were a special gift from The Creator. Even during tribal battles over territory or stolen horses, it was customary for the sacred "smoking waters" to be a neutral zone where all could freely be healed. Back then, hot springs belonged to everyone, and understandably, we would like to believe that nothing has changed.

The Native American tradition of free access to hot springs was initially imitated by the pioneers. However, as soon as mineral water was perceived to have some commercial value, the new settlers' private property laws were invoked at most of the hot spring locations. Histories often include bloody battles with "white men" over hot spring ownership, and there are colorful legends about Indian curses that had dire effects for decades on a whole series of ill-fated owners. After many fierce legal battles, and a few gun battles, some ambitious settlers were able to establish clear legal titles to the properties. Then it was up to the new owners to figure out how to turn their geothermal flow into cash flow.

Pioneering settlers dismissed as superstition the Native Americans' spiritual explanation of the healing power of a hot spring. However, those settlers did know from experience that it was beneficial to soak their bodies in mineral water, even if they didn't know why or how it worked. Commercial exploitation began when the owner of a private hot spring started charging admission, ending centuries of free access.

The shift from outdoor soaks to indoor soaks began when proper Victorian customers demanded privacy. Then, affluent city dwellers, as they became accustomed to indoor plumbing and modern sanitation, were no longer willing to risk immersion in a muddy-edged, squishy-bottomed mineral spring, even if they believed that such bathing would be good for their health. Furthermore, they learned to like their urban comforts too much to trek to an outdoor spring in all kinds of weather. Instead, they wanted a civilized method of "taking the waters," and the great spas of Europe provided just the right model for American railroad tycoons and land barons to follow and to surpass.

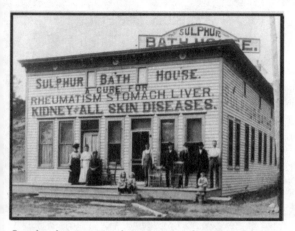

In the late 1800s farmers, ranchers, merchants, immigrants and gold seekers all came to the Black Hills of the Dakota Territory. Called Minnekahta (warm waters) by the original settlers, the town's name was changed to Hot Springs in 1886. Bath houses offering the healing powers of the warm springs were built over the many groups of small springs. While this building is no longer standing, the current *Springs Bath House* now takes its place.

Around the beginning of the 20th century, American hot spring resorts fully satisfied the combined demands of Victorian prudery, modern sanitation, and indoor comfort by offering separate men's and women's bathhouses with private individual porcelain tubs, marble shower rooms, and central heating. Scientific mineral analysis of the geothermal water was part of every resort's merchandising program, which included flamboyant claims of miraculous cures and glowing testimonials from medical doctors. Their promotional material also featured social amenities, such as luxurious suites, sumptuous restaurants, and grand ballrooms.

In recent decades, patronage of these resorts has declined, and many have closed down because the traditional medical claims were outlawed and modern medical plans refuse to reimburse anyone for a mineral water "treatment." In the last few years the addition of spas at all of the large resorts, and also at many of the smaller commercial hot springs sites, has attracted a whole new generation of people who enjoy luxurious body treatments along with the hot water. A few of the larger resorts have added new facilities such as golf courses, conference and exhibition spaces, and fitness centers. The smaller hot spring establishments have responded to modern demand by installing larger (six people or more) communal soaking tubs and family-size soaking pools in private spaces and most now offer at least a masseuse on the premises.

In addition to the privately owned hot spring facilities, there are several dozen locations that are owned and operated by federal, state, county, or city agencies. States, counties, and cities usually staff and operate their own geothermal installations. Locations in US National Forests and National Parks are usually operated under contract by privately owned companies. The nature and quality of the mineral water facilities offered at these locations vary widely.

Although natural mineral water (from a spring or well) is required for a truly authentic traditional "therapeutic soak," there is a new generation of dedicated soakers who will not patronize a motel unless it has a hot pool. They know full well that the pool is filled with gas-heated tap water and treated with chlorine, but it is almost as good as the real thing and a lot more convenient. We chose to include in our hunt for hot water those locations that offer private-space hot tubs for rent by the hour.

According to California legend, the historic redwood tub was invented by a Santa Barbara group who often visited Big Caliente Hot Springs. One evening, a member of the group wished out loud that they could have their delicious outdoor communal soaks without having to endure the long dusty trips to and from the springs. Another member of the group suggested that a large redwood wine cask might be used as an alternate soaking pool in the city. It was worth a try, and it was a success. Over time, other refugees from the long Big Caliente drive began to build their own group soaking pools from wine casks, and the communal hot tub era was born.

The original indoor pool and some of the guests at *Chico Hot Springs*, Montana.

9

USING THIS GUIDE

The primary tool in this guide is the KEY MAP, which is provided for each state or geographical subdivision. The KEY MAP INDEX on the outside back cover tells the page number where each of the KEY MAPS can be found. Each KEY MAP includes significant cities and highways, but please note that it is designed to be used with a standard highway map.

Within every KEY MAP, each location has been assigned a number that is printed next to the identifying circle or square. On the pages following the KEY MAP you will find descriptions of each location listed in numerical order.

The Master Alphabetical Index of Mineral Water Locations is printed at the end of the book and gives the page number on which each location description will be found. If you know the specific hot spring name, this alphabetical index is the place to start.

The following section describes the quick-read symbols that are used on the KEY MAPS and in the location descriptions.

● **Natural Locations with Minor Improvements**

On the key maps and in each hot spring listing, a solid round dot is used to indicate a natural hot spring, or hot well, where no fee (or minimal fee) is required and pools are generally created by the rearranging of rocks or by using other materials, such as cement, to create a place to soak (bathtubs and stock tanks qualify). At a few remote locations, you may be asked for a donation to help maintain the spring, or to pay a parking fee.

■ **Commercial Mineral Water Establishments**

On the key maps in this book and in the hot springs listings, a solid square is used to indicate a mineral water commercial location. A phone number and address are provided for the purpose of obtaining rates, additional information, and reservations.

❑ **Tubs Using Gas-heated Tap Water or Well Water**

Listings of rent-a-tub locations, indicated by a white square, begin with an overall impression of the premises and with the general location, usually within a city area. Premises are described. Nearly all locations require reservations, especially during the busy evening and weekend hours.

HOT SPRINGS ETIQUETTE

A Word about Nudity

You had best start with the hard fact that any private property owner, county administration, park superintendent, or forest supervisor has the authority to prohibit "public nudity" in a specific area or in a whole park or forest. Whenever the authorities have to deal with repeated complaints about nude bathers at a specific hot spring, it is likely that the area will be posted with NO NUDITY ALLOWED signs, and you could get a citation without further warning.

The vast majority of natural hot springs on public property are not individually posted, but most jurisdictions have some form of general regulation prohibiting public nudity. However, there have been some recent court cases establishing that a person could not be found guilty of indecent exposure if he removed his clothes only after traveling to a remote area where there was no one to be offended.

In light of these court cases, one of the largest national forests has retained its general "nude bathing prohibited" regulation but modified its enforcement procedure to give a nude person an opportunity to put on a bathing suit before a complaint can be filed or a violation notice issued.

In practical terms, this means that a group at an unposted hot spring can mutually agree to be nude. As soon as anyone else arrives and requests that all present put on bathing suits, those who refuse that request risk a citation. If you are in the nude group, all you need from the newcomers is some tolerance. You may be pleasantly surprised at the number of people who are willing to agree to a policy of clothing optional if, in a friendly manner, you offer them an opportunity to say "Yes."

In a separate section titled "For the Naturist" we have included a special listing of landed clubs in those states where there are hot springs to give skinnydippers alternatives to conventional motels/hotels/resorts. Most of the nudist/naturist resorts specifically prohibit bathing suits in their pools and have a policy of clothing optional elsewhere on the grounds. Most nudist/naturist resorts are not open to the public for drop-in visits, but the resorts listed in this book are often willing to offer a visitor's pass if you phone ahead and make arrangements.

Common Sense and Safety Tips

Respect is the key word when considering using a wilderness hot spring–respect for both the water and the area surrounding it, and for the people using it. Safety is also a key issue. The following guidelines will help make your soak safe and enjoyable.

It's Hot: Always, always check the temperature of the water before entering. Even if you have been to a spring several times, conditions affecting water flow and temperature change constantly.

It's Smelly or Not: Structures built over hot springs often prevent natural gasses from escaping. These can often build up and cause you to become dizzy and pass out. Be extremely cautious about staying within structures for any length of time.

Heads Up: Because many forms of bacteria and other organisms live in hot water, it is recommended by many that you do not put your head in the water.

Check it Out: If there is a ranger station in the area it is a good idea to talk to someone in the office to check for back country weather conditions, to see if any permits are needed, get maps, and make sure you have appropriate and sufficient supplies for your hike.

Over the River: The roads to many of the hot springs are often very primitive, cross deep washes, and are heavily rutted; stay on the roadway. Make sure your vehicle can make the trip. It is also often necessary for you to walk across running rivers to get to a springs. Cross at a wide, shallow spot that isn't above rapids or falls in case you get pulled downstream. Test rocks and logs before putting your weight on them. Face upstream while crossing and unbuckle the waiststraps of your backpack. Use a stick to increase stability.

The Gang's All Here: This is where consideration for other soakers comes in. If you arrive at a full pool, ask how long they plan on staying; or ask if you may join them. If you're the first person there, invite others to join you. You'd be amazed at the interesting people you meet. If people are waiting for you to get out before they get in, determine a reasonable length of time, and leave when agreed upon. Take a walk, watch the sky, read a book, and return later.

Cry of the Wild: Dogs go with their owners, and kids go along with their parents. It is up to the adults in this situation to take care of their children and their pets. Dogs do not belong in the pools, and loud barking is intrusive on an otherwise quiet time. As most of us know, when going to the bathroom in the wilderness, it is necessary to go off the trail 200 feet and away from the rivers and springs. This also holds true for your animals. Clean up after your pet. Bring a leash and use it if necessary; some areas require that you do.

It's a wonderful thing to introduce children to wilderness activities. However, as with any outdoor activity, particularly ones involving water, and often very hot water, close supervision is necessary. This is a great opportunity to teach children to respect nature and others.

No-Nos: Sex–No! Glass–No!

Everything in Moderation: Alcohol (follow posted signs and local ordinances; use common sense).

Rub-a-dub-dub: While some springs actually use a bathtub as a soaking pool, they are not the place to wash yourself, your clothes, or your cooking utensils. Soap, shampoo, detergent, and toothpaste really mess up the water.

It's Mine: Some of the hot springs in the book are on private property, and sometimes it is necessary to cross private land to get to a spring. Be particularly courteous when encountering these situations if you want to be able to continue to use these lands. Close all gates you need to open, stay on marked trails and roads, leave it cleaner than when you found it, and, if stated, ask permission before entering the area or the springs. Behave responsibly so that the springs will remain open.

CAUTION

NATURAL HOT SPRINGS

- **Water temperatures vary by site, ranging from warm to very hot . . . 180°F.**

- **Prolonged immersion may be hazardous to your health and result in hyperthermia (high body temperature).**

- **Footing around hot springs is often poor. Watch out for broken glass. Don't go barefoot and don't go alone. Please don't litter.**

- **Elderly persons and those with a history of heart disease, diabetes, high or low blood pressure, or who are pregnant should consult their physician prior to use.**

- **Never enter hot springs while under the influence of: alcohol, anti-coagulants, antihistamines, vasodilators, hypnotics, narcotics, stimulants, tranquilizers, vasoconstrictors, anti-ulcer or anti-Parkinsonian medicines. Undesirable side effects such as extreme drowsiness may occur.**

- **Hot springs are naturally occurring phenomena and as such are neither improved nor maintained by the Forest Service.**

CARING FOR THE OUTDOORS

This is an enthusiastic testimonial and an invitation to join in supporting the work of the US Forest Service, the National Park Service, and the several State Park Services.

Nearly all usable primitive hot springs are in national forests, and many commercial hot spring resorts are surrounded by a national forest. Even if you will not be camping in one of their excellent campgrounds, we recommend that you obtain official Forest Service maps for all of the areas through which you will be traveling. Maps may be purchased from the Forest Service regional offices listed below. To order by mail, phone or write for an order form, or go to their web site: www.fs.fed.us

Northern Region   406 329-3675
(No. Idaho, Montana, So. Dakota)
Federal Bldg., PO Box 7669, Misssoula, MT 59807

Rocky Mountain Region   303 275-5350
(Eastern Wyoming, So. Dakota, Colorado)
740 Simms St., Lakewood, CO 80401

Intermountain Region   801 625-5306
(So. Idaho, Utah, Nevada, and Western Wyoming)
324 25th St., Ogden, UT 84401

Pacific Northwest Region   503 808-2644
(Washington, Oregon)
333 SW First Ave., Portland, OR 97208

Alaska Region   907 586-8806
Regional Office PO Box 21628
Juneau, AK 99802-1628

When you arrive at a national forest, head for the nearest ranger station and let them know what you would like to do in addition to putting your body in hot mineral water. If you plan to stay in a wilderness area overnight, request information about wilderness permits and camping permits. Discuss your understanding of the dangers of water pollution, including giardia (back country dysentery) with the Forest Service staff. They are good friends as well as competent public servants.

Note: Fire regulations change frequently during the season. Check with the local Forest Service as to whether camp fires are permitted or not. You can be sited and fined for illegal use of fire.

Leave No Trace

Plan ahead: Whenever you travel into the wilderness areas be sure to leave word with friends as to your exact destination. Read the signs at the trailhead for any new information and where they have a registration book, use it. In case you do get lost, search and rescue teams will have a start in locating you. Know the regulations for the area you are entering.

Take a good orienteering class and know basic first aid. Carry a compass and purchase a topo map for the area.

Watch the weather: Always check with the local authorities before you start out.

High elevations: Acclimate yourself before you hike. Drink plenty of water. If you experience any symptoms such as dizziness, severe headaches, etc., head back down.

Don't cut switchbacks: A little less time to your destination is not worth ruining fragile vegetation. In areas with no trails, try to walk on firm surfaces and avoid cutting a new trail.

Respect: archeological, historical, or natural items. It's against Federal law to remove them. Don't go into old mining structures as they are unstable and dangerous.

Camping: Select a previously used campsite. Camp away from the trails and at least 200 feet from lakes and streams. Keep campsites small and focus on areas without vegetation. Avoid places where impacts are just beginning.

Clean up: Set up camp, wash dishes, and bathe at least 200 feet from water (this is especially necessary near hot springs). Use biodegradable soap or no soap; soil and pine needles or dry sand make great scouring pads for dishes. Separate leftover food and bag it to take back. Scatter gray water away from water sources and camp sites. Don't bury trash (animals dig it up).

Campfires: Try to avoid building campfires in high-use areas where wood is scarce. If you do build a fire, use existing fire rings and make sure to burn all remaining pieces of wood and charcoal down to white ashes. Soak with water and crush any remnants. Or better yet, bring a small gas stove.

Bury human waste: Dig six-inch-deep holes at least 200 feet from camp, trails, and water. Carry out toilet paper in doubled plastic bags (wild animals will dig up buried paper).

Nick Hertelendy

Whether camping in the desert or the mountains, or sharing a hot spring where some are clothed and some are not, respect for the environment and for each other is the key to a successful time in the wilderness which you can repeat over and over.

Pack it in, pack it out: Avoid burning trash. To do so takes an intense fire, almost always leaving bits and pieces that will not burn. Don't bury trash. Animals, time, and erosion will unearth it.

Leave the area cleaner than when you found it.

Leave No Trace is a non-profit organization dedicated to inspiring responsible outdoor recreation by teaching and promoting minimum impact practices. They offer for sale items relating to this philosophy to help you maintain and protect our open spaces and wildlands. I encourage you to get their brochures for the specific area, or type of area, you will be hiking in before you set out. Their web site is www.LNT.org, and their phone is 800 332-8100.

Phil Wilcox

THE SEVEN PRINCIPLES OF LEAVE NO TRACE

Plan Ahead and Prepare
Travel and Camp on Durable Surfaces
Dispose of Waste Properly
Leave What You Find
Minimize Campfire Impacts
Respect Wildlife
Be Considerate of Other Visitors

ALASKA

See page 15 for map of hot springs outside of Nome, Alaska (50A-B).

AK 11
AK 2   52
51
AK 6   53
54
Fairbanks

Dawson City

ALASKA
YUKON TERRITORY

AK 2

AK 3

AK 1

ALASKA HIGHWAY

Anchorage

AK 4

101

Whitehorse

BC 97

YUKON   TERRITORY
BRITISH   COLUMBIA

102

Pacific Ocean

Juneau

BRITISH COLUMBIA
ALASKA

56
55
57
Sitka
58
59

BC 37

BC 16

BC 16
103
Prince
Rupert
104

This map was designed to be used with a standard highway map.

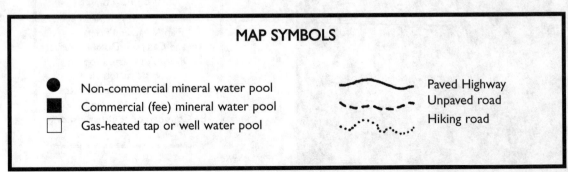

MAP SYMBOLS

● Non-commercial mineral water pool
■ Commercial (fee) mineral water pool
□ Gas-heated tap or well water pool

〜 Paved Highway
--- Unpaved road
··· Hiking road

Photos by Oscar Voss

The springs are on Catholic Church property, which includes the remains of a Catholic mission. Before the mission there was a resort here that sprang up around 1900 that offered baths, a saloon, and a dance hall for local miners. Traces of the old bathhouses still remain.

50A   PILGRIM HOT SPRINGS

● **North of the city of Nome**

A sixty mile trip on rough gravel roads requiring a high-clearance vehicle (or an airplane as there is a small landing strip) takes you to the one tub, situated out in the middle of an open field surrounded by a shelter. Access depends on whether one of the resident caretakers is around to let you on the property (there is no phone so you can not call ahead). A stand of trees between the tub and caretakers' compound provides some privacy. Open in the summer only until 8 PM. You must be admitted by the caretaker.

Scalding mineral water is piped to a plastic-lined tub, the excess running off into the fields. A ladder is provided to climb down into the water which is about shoulder high. Water temperature is about 111 plus degrees in the tub. Bathing suits required.

Directions: From Nome, take the Nome-Taylor Road north of town, 53.6 miles (watch the milemarkers on the east side of the road). Turn left at the unmarked and sometimes rough side road (not the second side road a little north of mile 53.6) and continue about eight miles to the end of the road where hopefully one of the caretakers will be there to let you onto the property. Allow two hours each way between Nome and the Pilgrim entrance. Once on the property, it's about a 10 minute walk down a sometimes muddy road to a compound with several buildings. Go into the compound, stay to the left of an old church, turning left past the first red building to pick up the trail to the tub.

GPS: N 65 05.580 W 164 55.320

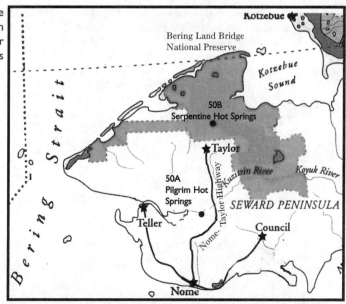

Inupiat Eskimos call this place Iyat, meaning "cooking pot" or "a site for cooking."

50B   SERPENTINE HOT SPRINGS

● North of the city of Nome

Surrounded by strangely shaped outcrops or "Tors." and used for thousands of years by the local villagers the hot springs is located in one of the remote valleys in the Bering Land Bridge National Preserve situated on the Seward Peninsula. Accessible only be plane. The area is subject to severe weather. Come prepared.

A wooden tub for bathing is enclosed in a small bathhouse where water temperatures can range from 140-170° and can be cooled by adding snow in the winter or waiting for it to cool naturally in the summer

A bunkhouse-style cabin sleeps fifteen to twenty people in two sections. All cabins are unreserved. Camping is relatively unrestricted, with no formal campsites and no developed water, power, or sanitation facilities. Nearest services are back in Nome and Kotzebue.

Air taxi services provide scheduled flight to neighboring villages or charter flights into the Preserve. Some of the small villages offer limited clothing, food, or supplies and also offer meals and lodging during tourist season. In summer access is by bush planes or small boats. In winter you will need small planes on skis, snowmachines, and dog sleds. The western boundary of the National Preserve lies only forty-two miles from the Bering Strait.

While the National Park Service and the Bering land Bridge National Preserve are officially in charge of the springs, it is your responsibility to care for this precious resource.

Note: If you are interested in traveling to this remote location contact the Park Service in Anchorage at 970 257-2687 and make sure to go to their website at www.nps.gov/bela/index.htm. The Preserve headquarters in Nome offers additional and up-to-date information on weather and travel conditions.

GPS: N 65 51.480 W 164 42.600

People of this area hunt, trap, bathe, and conduct traditional healing practices near the hot springs. Inupiat traditions say that the valley is the home of powerful spirits. The site is a rest stop and shelter for winter travelers.

51 MANLEY HOT SPRINGS
PO Box 50   907 672-3171
Manley Hot Springs, AK 99756

A unique geothermal greenhouse containing three cement soaking tubs in addition to many flowers and organic vegetables. Located in an area of thick birch and spruce forests with abundant wildlife. Elevation 330 feet. Open all year.

Natural mineral water flows out of two springs (125° and 136°) and is piped to the greenhouse for space heating and for use in the soaking pools. Temperatures of 80-100° are ideally maintained in the three pools which are drained, refilled, and sanitized each day so no chemical treatment of the water is needed. Tub temperatures can not be individually controlled and are often too hot or too cold to soak in. Tubs are handicap accessible with assistance. Bathing suits optional.

While there are no services on the premises, there are very comfortable accommodations (rooms and log cabins) heated by the hot water, a restaurant and lounge at the nearby Manley Roadhouse (907 672-3161) Hunting, boating, and fishing are readily available nearby. Fuel and a general store are just around the corner. A 2,700 foot air strip is nearby. Credit cards accepted at the Roadhouse and the general store.

For information, rates, or reservations contact Charles or Gladys Dart at the above number.

The tubs are in a hothouse which also grows delicious tomatoes and other vegetables.

El Dorado Hot Springs

Directions: Take the Steese Highway north from Fairbanks 11 miles to Fox and turn onto the Elliott Highway. At mile 79, the Elliott makes a sharp left turn (don't miss it) and continue to the hot springs.

Note: It is 118 miles to Manley from Fairbanks. Be sure to fill your gas tank full at both ends of your trip and make sure you have supplies with you "just in case." Once you leave the main highway you have about 80 miles to traverse, about 70 of which are on gravel and can be quite rough.

Courtesy of Manley Hot Springs

The road ends here at this outpost. Manley was founded in 1902 and hasn't changed much since then. People come in and out by dog sled and snowmobile, or plane in the winter as the roads are not plowed. Besides rooms and cabins at reasonable rates, be prepared to enjoy the delicious homestyle cooking.

Tom DeLong

52 TOLOVANA HOT SPRINGS, LTD
PO Box 83058   907 455-6706
■   Fairbanks, AK 99708
www.mosquitonet.com/~tolovana

Two remote and rustic cabins with outdoor cedar soaking tubs surrounded by spruce, birch and aspen forests, one-hundred road miles north of Fairbanks. Elevation: 800 feet. Open all year; by reservation only.

Natural mineral water flows out of many geothermal springs at 135° and collects in a settling pond that maintains a temperature of 100°. Water from each of these two sources is piped to the two widely separated soaking tubs, allowing complete control of tub water temperature. The apparent local custom is clothing optional.

The two fully outfitted cabins are the only services available on the premises. Bring your own food and sleeping bag. There is a remote air strip two miles from the cabins, and it is eleven miles by all-year trail to the nearest road. It is thirty-five miles to a phone, gas, and an air strip at Minto Village. Local air charters are available. Phone for guided dog sled, snow-machine, or ski trips. Phone for rates, reservations, and weather conditions. No credit cards are accepted.

While a soak surrounded by nature's winter wonderland is magical, it would be wise to heed the words in the Tolovana Hot Springs brochure: "The trails to Tolovana Hot Springs are for the adventurous. Experience is recommended for winter travel." Even in summer it is still an eleven-mile hike, unless, of course, you charter a plane and fly in. Then the hike is only two miles.

REMOTE NATURAL HOT SPRINGS

Arctic Circle Hot Springs Resort

53 ARCTIC CIRCLE HOT SPRINGS
PO Box 30069   907 520-5113
■   Central, AK 99730

Delightful historic resort hotel and cabins with a large outdoor swimming pool and several private-space pools in the hotel and cabins, 134 miles northeast of Fairbanks. Elevation 900 feet. Open all year.

Natural mineral water flows out of a spring at 139° and is piped to an outdoor Olympic-size swimming pool and to individual hydropools in four cabins, one hydropool in the honeymoon suite and one hydropool on each of the three main floors of the hotel. The swimming pool is maintained at 105°, with a minimum of chlorination. Day use is available at the swimming pool and in the three hotel hydropools. The pools area, deck, and cabins are handicap accessible with some assistance. Bathing suits are required in the swimming pool.

Hotel rooms, cabins (some with full kitchens), flat space for tents and RVs, a community room for sleeping bags, dining room, saloon, ice-cream parlor (summer), exercise room, massage, and library are available on the premises. Geothermal energy is used to heat all rooms and cabins. All types of hunting and fishing are located nearby and tours can be arranged. A 3,600 foot lighted airstrip is nearby. It is eight miles to all other services in Central. Credit cards accepted.

The road ends above *Arctic Circle Hot Springs*. It is the furthest north one can drive in the United States, except Prudhoe Bay. Only fifty miles from the Arctic Circle, it is light out twenty-four hours a day in the summer. A great place to see the Northern Lights.

Directions: From Fairbanks, drive north on Steese Highway, then east on AK 6 to Central, and east for 8 miles on Hot Springs Road to the resort. Of the 134 miles from Fairbanks, 88 miles are on dirt road. Again, be prepared for emergencies. Phone for information on rates, reservations, and road conditions.

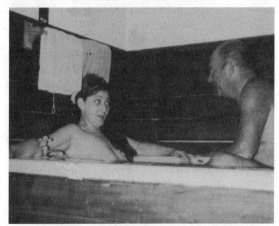

El Dorado Hot Spring

Mineral water fills not only a swimming pool, but the cabins have their own tubs big enough for two.

It would be worth the trip to Alaska just to soak in this beautiful hot natural mineral water lake.

54 CHENA HOT SPRINGS
PO Box 58740   907 451-8104
■   Fairbanks, AK 99707   800 478-4681
www.chenahotsprings.com

Comfortable lodge or cabins, an indoor swimming pool, soaking pools, two whirlpools and an outdoor warm lake. Located on 440 acres of pristine wilderness in a wooded valley fifty-seven miles east of Fairbanks. Elevation 1,200 feet. Open all year.

Natural mineral water flows out of four springs at temperatures up to 156° and is piped to several pools that are treated with chlorine, except the outdoor lake. The glassed-in swimming pool is maintained at 90°; the indoor soaking pool and the two indoor whirlpools are maintained at 100-104°. The new pool building includes a deck containing an outdoor hydrojet pool. A new adult-only outdoor rock lake that is maintained at 104° has also been added. All pools are available for day use as well as for registered guests. Bathing suits are required.

Seventy-two comfortable hotel rooms, eight suites and eight cabins, RV hookups (electricity, dump station) and tent sites, laundry, restaurant, and bar, and a 3,500 foot airstrip are available on the premises. Activities on the grounds include horseback riding, sleigh rides, dog cart rides (summer), dog mushing (winter), cross-country skiing, aurora viewing, fishing, volleyball, gold panning, biking, hiking, canoeing, raft trips, snowmobiling, snow coach cruises, ice skating, and snow shoeing. A "flightseeing" tour can be arranged. Massage is also available. It is fifty-seven miles to all other services in Fairbanks. Major credit cards accepted.

Directions: From Fairbanks, go north on Steese Highway and the east on Chena Hot Springs Road (paved) to the resort. Phone for rates, specials and reservations, or see our website.

Among the popular activities at Chena Hot Springs, besides soaking in the hot water, are viewing the spectacular Northern Lights and the wildlife that often wanders through the property and the many artifacts that have been collected over the years.

■   In the town of Tenakee Springs

A wooden bathhouse containing a concrete soaking pool, built over a hot spring in a tiny, rural Alaskan village with no cars or roads. Elevation is sea level. Open all year.

Natural mineral water flows out of the spring at 108°, directly up into a five-foot by ten-foot concrete container that was built to keep out the sea water at high tide. Men and women are assigned different hours of the day. Bathing suits and soap are prohibited in the pool. Donations are accepted in the adjoining store.

There are no services available on the premises, but rooms, bunkhouse, bar, and laundry are offered nearby in the nostalgic Victorian Tenakee Inn, 800 327-9347. A restaurant and curio shop are located nearby.

The Alaska Marine Highway Ferry stops for only fifteen minutes at Tenakee Springs, which is located on the north shore of Tenakee Inlet on Chichagof Island, forty five miles southwest of Juneau.

Tenakee Hot Springs is the main attraction in a town with no cars and single gravel street. The wooden bathhouse has separate hours set aside for men and women throughout the day.

Photo by Katie Corbin

56   WHITE SULPHUR HOT SPRINGS

●   **Northwest of the city of Sitka**

Remote hot spring pools with a nearby rentable National Forest Service cabin, within a beautiful wilderness area of the West Chichagof Wilderness Area in the Tongass National Forest, sixty-five miles from Sitka. Elevation 50 feet. Open all year.

Natural mineral water flows out of one spring at 111°, supplying a natural-bottom, outdoor, primitive soaking pool. A three-sided log structure has been built directly over another spring. The pool is in a natural rock depression, approximately four-feet deep. The open side of this shelter, which can be slid open, provides a spectacular view of Pacific Ocean waves crashing on rocky cliffs. Whether to wear a bathing suit or not is determined by the mutual agreement of those present.

There are no services available on the premises, but camping is available on open wilderness land which also provides hiking trails. A forest service cabin behind the bathhouse has firewood, bunks, etc. Access is only by boat, plus a one-mile hike from Mirror Harbor. For cabin reservations call toll-free 877 444-6777; or on the internet: ReserveUSA.com. For charter boat rental, and a detailed map to the springs, contact the US Forest Service, 204 Siginaka Way, Sitka, AK 99835. 907 747-6671.

GPS: N 57 48.420 W 136 20.460

Lisianski Inlet Wilderness Lodge and Charters, a family owned concern, offers a variety of trips and charters from something as simple as a hot springs drop-off and pick-up to fully guided Alaskan Safaris. The lodge provides comfortable, spacious rooms, or a private beach cabin with its own kitchen and bath. Meals are included in the price and consist of a variety of traditional Alaskan fare.

Pick up for the hot springs trips is from Pelican. It takes about an hour. You can use the state ferry to get to Pelican which only gets there every two weeks in the summer.

They can be contacted at PO Box 765, Pelican, Alaska 99832. 800 962-8441.

If it is too cold to sit outside you can get an unrestricted view of the bay and the ocean from the three-sided shelter pictured below. Of added interest are the carvings on the walls of names of past visitors, fishing boats, and items of interest.

Photos courtesy of Lisianski Inlet Lodge

Photos by Oscar Voss

57   BARANOF WARM SPRINGS

● **East of the city of Sitka**

Three outdoor pools about a fifteen minute hike uphill from the village of Baranof on Warm Springs Bay. Situated next to chilly rapids and offering views of the the bay. Surrounded by the beautiful green trees of the Tongass National Forest. Elevation slightly above sea level. Open all year.

Hot mineral water with a faint sulphur smell flows from the source spring into two adjacent knee-deep rock-and-silt pools, each about 110° and with room for several bathers. Some of the hot water flows into a small 108° rock pool a few feet way next to a cold stream rushing toward Warm Springs Bay. This waist-deep, slick-sided pool has room for one person standing up, plus a very good friend squeezed in sideways. Bring a swimsuit, as these pools are popular with both local families and boaters stopping by Baranof village.

Baranof Wilderness Lodge and a general store, about one-half mile away, operate during the summer.

Directions from the boat or floatplane landing: From town follow the boardwalk where it takes a sharp right turn uphill toward some houses. The easy trail continues straight ahead. Within ten minutes you will find a turnoff to the left, marked with a sign pointing to the springs. A few minutes later, the rough side trail will end at the pools. Bring boots—the trail is often quite muddy and during the winter you will definitely encounter snow. For more information contact the Sitka Convention and Visitors Bureau, PO Box 1226, Sitka, AK 99835, 907 747-5940.

GPS: N 57 05.100 W 134 50.340

A short walk will take you to the pools located behind the village. The rapids in the photo on the left flow into the waterfall shown below

To get to the springs by floatplane from Sitka:
    Harris Aircraft, 907 966-3050.
To get to the springs by boat from Sitka:
    Alaskan Fishing Eagle Boat Charters, Captain Tom
    Smotherman, 907 747-6759.

Photos by Oscar Voss

58   GODDARD HOT SPRINGS

● **South of the city of Sitka**

Two modern cedar soaking tubs in open shelters overlooking beautiful Hot Springs Bay and located on City of Sitka land on the outer coast of Baranof Island. Elevation 30 feet. Open all year.

Natural mineral water flows out of a spring at 153° and is piped to a double faucet on each of two tubs, one uphill from the cove, and the other next to the water. Cold water is also piped to that faucet, permitting complete control of the tub water temperature. Two to four can sit comfortably on the ledge inside each tub. There is no charge for using the facilities which are owned and maintained by the City of Sitka. A primitive squishy-bottom knee-deep warm pool, about 100° is found on a short, but muddy trail into the woods just past the upper pool. Whether to wear a bathing suit or not is determined by the mutual agreement of those present.

Boardwalks and stairs have been constructed and camping is permitted in the open spaces, although the usual dampness of the area can make for uncomfortable camping. There are no other services available on the premises. Access is possible only by charter boat or by float plane in good weather. For more information, contact the Sitka Convention and Visitors Bureau, PO Box 1226, Sitka, AK 99835, 907 747-5940.

GPS: N 56 50.160 W 135 22.440

Goddard Hot Springs provides a beautiful view of peaceful Hot Springs Bay from one of the tubs. The walkways and stairs put in by the City of Sitka provide access to the tubs, while a short, but muddy trail, that branches off the boardwalk takes you to this warm pool which is cooler and less crowded.

● **North of the village of Wrangell**

Two large wooden tubs located along the base of a steep, glaciated, granite cliff surrounded by willow and stands of Sitka spruce and hemlock, thirty miles up the Stikine River within the Stikine-LeConte Wilderness of the Tongass National Forest. Elevation 25 feet. Recommended June to October.

Natural mineral water emerges from beneath boulders at the base of a cliff at approximately 120° and is piped to a large wooden tub enclosed in a post and beam structure with insect screening. The other tub is in an open structure overlooking the meadow. Water temperature is controlled by adjusting the hot and cold water pipes. Whether to wear a bathing suit or not is determined by the mutual agreement of those present. There is considerable traffic evenings and weekends, so please use discretion, and whatever you pack in, pack out.

Changing rooms, a picnic table, fire ring, benches, and outdoor privies are available on the premises. The nearest public recreation cabins (reservations required) are within three miles. All other services are back in Wrangell or Telegraph Creek, BC.

Access is by small, shallow draft boat via Hot Springs Slough, a tributary of Ketili Slough, a side channel of the Stikine River, twenty-eight miles from Wrangell. Ease of access depends on river level; during river levels of less than sixteen feet*, access by watercraft may be limited. It is also possible to fly into Telegraph Creek, BC, and to kayak or motor boat down to the river's mouth. While the rapids are not difficult, there is much submerged material in the river, making it a challenge for beginners. It is recommended that you follow someone down the river the first time; and travel with several spare props and a pole. For cabin reservations call toll-free 877 444-6777; or on the internet: ReserveUSA.com. For information on charter flights, boat rentals, and detailed directions to the spring, contact the US Forest Service, Tongass National Forest, Wrangell Ranger District, PO Box 51, Wrangell, AK 99929, 907 874-2323. They also have wonderful maps and printed information.

Source map: USGS *Petersburg C-1* topographic map.
GPS: N 56 43.020 W 132 00.300

*The Stikine River level is posted on the internet by the USGS at: http://www-water-ak.usgs.gov/rt-cgi/gen_stn_pg?station=15024800

Information and photos courtesy of David Rak, USDA-FS, Wrangell Ranger District

Dating back to aboriginal times, this site was more recently developed by local citizens for their own use and is currently maintained by the National Forest Service. The trail to the springs begins at the low-water landing and, after a series of log staircases and a log stringer bridge, connects the upper, enclosed tub with the open-air structure below and then continues down to the high-water landing. Along with hot springs enthusiasts, black and brown grizzly bears, moose, wolf, and waterfowl visit the area.

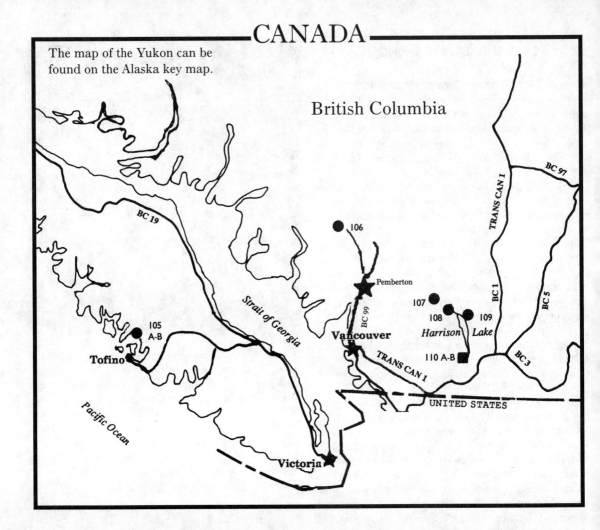

CANADA

The map of the Yukon can be found on the Alaska key map.

British Columbia

BC 19

106

Pemberton

BC 99

105 A-B

Tofino

Strait of Georgia

Vancouver

107

108 109

Harrison Lake

110 A-B

BC 1

BC 97

TRANS CAN 1

BC 5

BC 3

TRANS CAN 1

UNITED STATES

Pacific Ocean

Victoria

This map was designed to be used with a standard highway map.

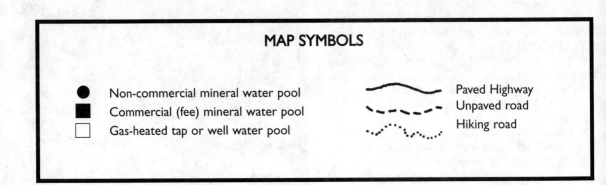

MAP SYMBOLS

● Non-commercial mineral water pool
■ Commercial (fee) mineral water pool
□ Gas-heated tap or well water pool

〜 Paved Highway
– – – Unpaved road
······ Hiking road

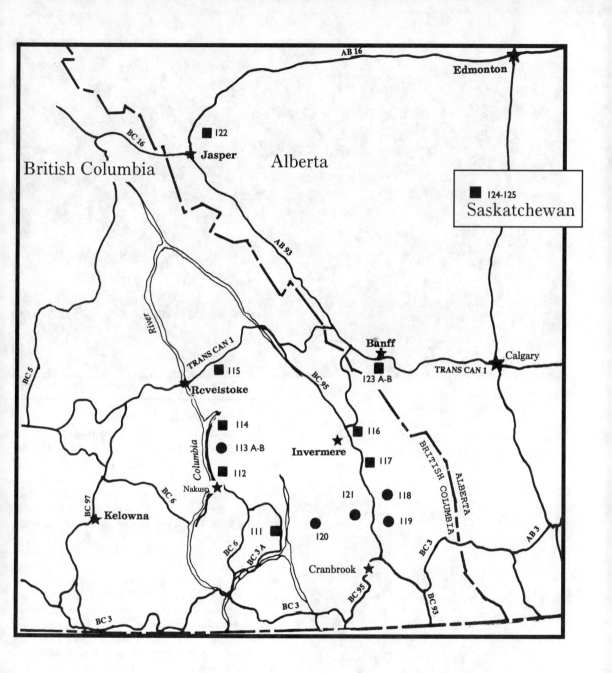

British Columbia

Alberta

Saskatchewan

Edmonton

AB 16

BC 16

■ 122

★ Jasper

AB 93

Banff ★

Calgary ★

TRANS CAN 1

■ 124-125

BC 5

TRANS CAN 1

■ 115

BC 95

■ 123 A-B

River

Revelstoke ●

Columbia

■ 114

● 113 A-B

■ 112

★ Invermere

■ 116

■ 117

BC 97

BC 6

Nakusp ★

● 118

● 119

BRITISH COLUMBIA

ALBERTA

Kelowna ★

BC 6

● 121

BC 3

AB 3

BC 3 A

■ 111

● 120

Cranbrook ★

BC 95

BC 93

BC 3

BC 3

Courtesy of Takhini Hot Springs

In the early 1900s trappers gained access to these springs, formed by volcanic action, via the old Dawson Trail or by the Takhini River. During the early 40s, when the Alaska Highway was being built, the US Army maintained greenhouses in the area.

Photo by Phil Wilcox

101 TAKHINI HOT SPRINGS
(shown on the Alaska key map)
PO Box 20404   867 633-2706
Whitehorse, Yukon, Y1A 7A2

Restaurant, campground, and mineral water pool in the scenic Takhini River valley. Daylight lasts from nineteen hours in June to just five and one-half hours in December. Elevation 2,400 feet. Open all year, but call first as hours vary considerably.

Natural mineral water flows out of a volcanic crater reservoir at 118° and is piped to a large outdoor pool, where it is mixed with cold water as needed to maintain a temperature of 102-104°. The pool is drained and refilled each day, so a minimum of chlorination is needed. Some handicap access. Bathing suits are required.

Restaurant, RV and tent campground, sauna, showers, laundromat, and horseback riding are available on the premises. It is seventeen miles to all other services in Whitehorse. Credit cards are accepted.

Directions: Northwest of Whitehorse on the Alaska Highway, turn north on YT 2 toward Dawson City. Drive 3 miles, then watch for the Takhini Hot Springs sign and turn west 6 miles to the springs.

Liard Hot Springs: A beautiful provincial park on the Alaska Highway with a six-foot-wide boardwalk wandering through a wetlands environment where you are likely to view over 250 boreal forest plants—several supported by the hot springs conditions. Wildlife is also prevalent. The Beta pool (above) provides a hot, deep soak and a swim. It was originally developed by the US Army in 1942.

102   LIARD RIVER HOT SPRINGS PROVINCIAL PARK
(shown on the Alaska key map)
■ Northwest of Muncho Lake, BC
wlapwww.gov.bc.ca/bcparks

A lovely, primitive geothermal pond and pool with convenient boardwalk access and a campground, adjoining the Alaska Highway near the Yukon border. Elevation 1,500 feet. Open all year.

Natural mineral water flows out of several springs at temperatures up to 120° directly into a large, shallow, natural pond (named Alpha) created by a low dam across the creek bed. The water cools to comfortable levels as it flows toward the spillway over the dam. Underwater benches are provided for soaking, and the shallow end of the pond is suitable for children. One side of the pond has been improved with stairs, a large deck, changing rooms, and toilets. A six-foot-wide boardwalk has been built through a wetlands environment from the parking area to the pond. Bathing suits required.

Five minutes beyond Alpha, along a dirt path, is a large natural pool (named Beta) that maintains a temperature of more than 100°. It also has stairs, a small deck, changing rooms, and toilets, but it is used primarily by adults because of the deep water.

Changer rooms and a playground are located on the premises. There is no charge for day use of the pools, but a fee is charged for sites in the campground. During the popular summer months, campsites fill early in the day. Sites can be reserved. There are no other services available. There is a cafe across the highway and a lodge within 0.5 miles. It is 41 miles to all other services. No credit cards accepted.

The park is located at mile marker 497 (765 km) on the Alaska Highway (BC 97) just below the Yukon Territory border. Follow the signs prominently displayed along the highway.

The dam pictured on the left creates the shallow Alpha pond that is ideal for children and soakers (shown on the right). Underwater benches are comfortable, and waterfalls are unique. Photos by Phil Wilcox

103 MOUNT LAYTON HOT SPRINGS RESORT (shown on the Alaska key map)
PO Box 550   250 798-2214
■ Terrace, BC V8G 4B5

A large, new 1,000-acre destination resort and water park in a beautiful setting on the edge of Lakelse Lake in Western British Columbia. Elevation 800 feet. Open all year.

Natural mineral water flows out of several springs at temperatures up to 186°, is treated with ozone, and is then piped to various pools and waterslides without requiring any other chemical treatment. The outdoor therapeutic pool is maintained at 103° and the outdoor main pool is maintained at 90°. Two of the three big waterslides exit into an indoor catch pool that is maintained at 90°. The third big waterslide exits outdoors into an arm of the main pool. There are also two short outdoor waterslides suitable for small children. Bathing suits are required.

Hotel rooms, dining room and restaurant, bar, and snack room are available on the premises. Fishing and boating are available at adjoining Lakelse Lake. It is 10 miles to all other services in Terrace. Visa, MasterCard, Diners, and American Express are accepted.

Directions: From Terrace, drive 14 miles south on BC 37 to the resort.

Photos by Phil Wilcox

Mount Layton: Three different waterslides can be reached in this tower. Children too small for these big slides have two slides of their own in the shallow end.

Two of the *Mount Layton* waterslides have an indoor catch pool so that fun can continue no matter what the outdoor weather is like.

Just one of the gorgeous vistas as you head up the channel.

Photos by Ron Thiele

104 DOUGLAS CHANNEL HOT SPRINGS
● (shown on the Alaska key map)

Eight different natural hot spring sites, some partially improved, along the edges of beautiful Douglas Channel. Accessible only by boat. Elevation sea level. Open all year.

The following three sites are the most popular.

Bishop Bay: One spring, 110°, 15 feet above high tide, supplies a three-foot by three-foot concrete bathhouse. Mooring buoys and a dock are in place.

Weewanie: One spring, 117°, 330 feet above sea level, supplies a small cement bathhouse, built with a grant from Crown Zellerbach.

Shearwater Point: Several springs, 113°, in a fractured rock wall supply a brick pool built by a lumber company for its employees in 1922.

The other sites are difficult to find and/or are flooded at high tide. For more information, contact the Kitimat Chamber of Commerce, PO Box 214, Kitimat, BC V8C 2G7. 250 632-6294, FAX 250 632-4685.

Directions: Kitimat is at the head of Douglas Channel, 36 miles south of Terrace on BC 37.

For those of you who like to sail, this whole area is a sailor's dream, and you can include a hot soak as well.

105A HOT SPRINGS COVE

● **Northwest of the town of Tofino, on Vancouver Island**

Unique confluence of geothermal runoff and ocean waves, located twenty-six nautical miles up the coast from Tofino in Maquinna Regional Park, reachable only by boat or floatplane. The springs offer a spectacular view of the ocean. Elevation 40 feet. Open all year.

Natural mineral water flows out of the main spring at 122°, providing a hot showerbath as it falls over a cliff edge. This geothermal water gradually cools as it flows through tiered boulder-lined soaking pools in a rocky channel leading to the ocean at temperatures of 107-110°. The incoming tide and wave action intermittently splash cold sea water over the visitors in the lower pools and the lowest pool tends to disappear during high tide. Clothing is optional although the remoteness of this location does not assure you of privacy and it would be a good idea to bring a suit. During summer weekends, you will have plenty of company, which insures a maximum of excitement when the icy waves surge into the tubs. While the walk to the cove (about one-half mile) is not strenuous there are quite a few stairs which may be a problem for both the elderly and the very young.

You will need to bring a picnic lunch, beverage, bathing suit and towel, good walking shoes, water shoes, sun gear, (light rain gear, if appropriate), a day pack, and your camera. Two restrooms and a changing room are located at the springs. Overnight camping near the springs is prohibited, but a private campground is located adjacent to the fishing boat pier (250 725-3318). Rooms are available in a lodge at a nearby Indian village (250 724-8570). For a list of accommodations call the Tofino Information Center at 250 725-3414 or visit their web site at tofinobc.org.

For information and reservations, contact Jamie's Whaling Station (250 725-3919, 800 667-9913). Based on our experience, they offer a really good trip, which is about six hours round trip. You might want to inquire about whale-watching trips (during certain seasons you are guaranteed a sighting), kayak adventures, and sailing cruises. You'll regret not having a camera.

To better enjoy your soak, plan on staying overnight at Clayoquot Sound's Hot Springs Lodge, owned and operated by Hesquiaht First Nation. Besides the usual amenities you will have access to a private beach. For lodging and Mathlahaw Water Taxi, phone 250 670-1106.

Note: You might want to ask around Tofino for information about Ahousal Hot Springs in the Gibson Marine Provincial Park on Flores Island.

Photos by Phil Wilcox

Hot Springs Cove not only has hot baths in the nooks and crannies between the rocks but lovely, warm water flows over the hillside offering a nice refreshing shower.

The view from the tub on the balcony is magnificent. Treat yourself to the two-story room that goes with it.

107   SKOOKUM
(LILLOOET)
● **North of the**

Three large, fibergla
near a logging road alor
feet. Open all year; ho
winter. Fee charged to

Natural mineral wa
Long pieces of PVC pip
eral water to a large fi
steel roofed A-frame. C
to carry a gravity flow
temperature within eac
hot and cold water. A
the third fiberglass tub
The use of bathing suit
those present.

112

■

of
agai
mou
(clo

awa
is tr
at 9
win
poo
Batl

cabi
cam
to
cre
and
vide
and
Hot
acc

Nak

.An
ing

105B   CABLE COVE INN
201 Main St.   800 663-6449
PO Box 339
❑   Tofino V0R 2Z0 British Columbia
www.cablecoveinn.com

Beautifully decorated, romantic inn with a magnificent view of Clayoquot Sound, Meares Island and Wickaninnish Island. Within walking distance of downtown Tofino. A wonderful place to stay before or after a trip to Hot Springs Cove. Elevation sea level. Open all year.

A Continental breakfast is included with the rental of one of the rooms and a shared, stocked kitchen is also available for your use. The "Honeymoon Suite" has a tub large enough for two, and the "Hot Tub Suite" with a second story loft, positions the hot tub out on a large deck with one of the best views of the sound. The remaining four rooms all have tubs with jets, and all rooms offer fireplaces and a view of the ocean. Rooms do not have televisions or telephones. Smoke-free facility. Adult oriented. No pets. One room is handicap accessible. Major credit cards accepted.

Call for additional information and reservations.

● **North**

The largest a
Columbia, surro
sources of hot
2,000 feet. Oper
ditions permittin
tions check with
604 898-2100. S

Water sour
springs area has
tions. New pool
ated on the low
walks and stairs
very fast flowing
swimming. The l
subject to flood
local custom.

A fully conta
No camping is
campground is
Meager Creek a
Creek Valley. A
south.

Directions: l
the Lillooet Fo
bridge over the
Coast Mountain
forest road for
and the Lillooet
head southwest
left and continu
ger Creek brid
here, as well as
to the pools. Ve
of Meager Cree
GPS: N 50.

Courtesy of Halcyon Hot Springs

---

114   HALCYON HOT SPRINGS
■   **PO Box 37**   **888 689-4699**
     Nakusp, BC V0G 1R0

A new destination resort where everything has to fit into nature and every tub will have a view of Mt. Odin and beautiful, forested surroundings. Elevation 1,900 feet. Open all year for overnight stays; hour and day passes also available.

Natural mineral water at 120° flows out of a hillside and is piped to a variety of pools. The hot spring soaking pool, with jets, is kept at 107°; the warm pool at 95°; and the large kidney-shaped swimming pool and children's pool at 85°. There is also a cold pool at 77°. If any chemicals need to be added it will be a minimal use of chlorine. Indoor theme rooms and a larger indoor mineral water pool are also available. The whole resort is handicap accessible. Bathing suits required.

One and two-bedroom chalets, fully furnished, overnight camping cabins, with or without bedding, and holding up to five people, thirty-five camping sites by the lake, and fifty fully serviced RV sites are on the premises. Changing rooms, a small bistro, restaurant, piano bar, gift shop, horseback riding and tours, ATV tours, 250 kilometers of trails, lake sports, and fishing are also being offered. Health services including massage, reflexology, and yoga are also available. Credit cards accepted.

Photos by Phil Wilcox

115   CANYON HOT SPRINGS
■   **PO Box 2400**   **250 837-2420**
     Revelstoke, BC V0E 2S0
     www.canyonhotsprings.com

Two hundred acres set in the spectacular Selkirk Mountains with creekside camping spaces and a magnificent view of the Monashee mountain range. Elevation 2,300 feet. Open May 15 to the end of September.

Natural mineral water is piped from Albert Canyon Spring at 87° and is gas-heated, as needed, and treated with chlorine. Two large outdoor swimming pools are maintained at 85°, the shallow one is perfect for children. The outdoor hot pool runs around 105°. The main pool deck and the pools are wheelchair accessible. Bathing suits required.

Locker rooms, cafe, gift shop, picnic area, laundry facilities, ten log cabins two family units, one chalet, 200 secluded RV and camping spots are available on the premises. Room rents include breakfast and use of springs; RV and camping spots do not. (Pool fees extra) It is twenty-three miles to a gas station in Revelstoke. Credit cards accepted.

Location: Twenty-three miles east of Revelstoke on Canada 1 between Revelstoke and Glacier National Parks.

116   RADIUM HOT SPRINGS

PO Box 40   250 347-9485
                                800 767-1611

■   **Radium Hot Springs, BC V0A 1M0**

Home to the Canadian Parks Service largest hot spring pool, with adjacent campground, and surrounded by the beautiful mountain scenery of Kootenay National Park where wildlife abounds. Elevation 2,800 feet. Open all year. Reduced rates mid-October to mid-April.

Natural mineral water flows out of several springs that are underneath and along the northeast wall of the hot pool and is collected and redistributed throughout the complex at a combined temperature of 114°. It is piped to two outdoor pools, where it is treated with chlorine. The swimming pool is maintained at a temperature of 84°, and the soaking pool is maintained at a temperature of 104°. A recently refurbished cool pool comes complete with diving board and a shallow lounging area perfect for children. The pool complex is fully wheelchair accessible. Bathing suits are required.

Changing rooms (some for families), bathing suit and towel rentals, massage, and a cafe are available on the premises along with a restaurant and a cafe at pool level. Pleiades Massage and Spa offers various types of therapies. Call for an appointment at 250 347-2100. Redstreak Provincial campground is located on a plateau above the pool complex, and a short trail leads down to the pool. Several other campgrounds are nearby, along with a lodge and restaurant. It is one and a-half miles to a store and service station in Radium. The Kootenay National Park Information Center is located in the building. Credit cards accepted.

Linda Nabon

117   FAIRMONT HOT SPRINGS RESORT
PO Box 10   250 345-6311
■ **Fairmont Hot Springs, BC V0B 1L0**

Famous, large destination resort and communal pool, located at the headwaters of the mighty Columbia River, beautifully landscaped and surrounded by the forested mountains of the Windermere Valley. Elevation 2,100 feet. Open all year.

Natural mineral water flows out of three springs at temperatures of 108°, 112° and 116° and is piped to the resort pools, where it is treated with chlorine and cooled with creek water as needed. The outdoor public plunge area, also available for day-use, includes a swimming pool, maintained from 87-90°, and a soaking pool maintained at 102°. An indoor soaking pool at 108°, an indoor cold plunge and another outdoor hot pool are reserved for hotel guests only. In addition, an old concrete and rock building on the hillside near the campsites has, what looks like, some of the original soaking tubs built in the early 1900s and still available to day-use customers. Some areas are handicap accessible. Bathing suits are required.

Locker rooms, massage, restaurants, conference center, spa services, store, service station, hotel rooms, full-service RV hookups, saddle horses, tennis, and golf are available on the premises with river rafting, skiing, and other seasonal sports nearby. Credit cards accepted.

Location: On BC 93, 64 miles north of Cranbrook and one-hundred miles south of Banff. The resort also has a private airport.

Hotel guests, campers, and day-use visitors have a variety of pools to soak in, including the old bath-house and outdoor pool (see below) dating back to the early 1900s when the resort was first opened.

Photos by Chris Andrews

A chain of rock-lined, sandy-bottom soaking pools along a gravel beach on the scenic Lussier River.

118   LUSSIER HOT SPRINGS

● **South of the village of Canal Flats**

A wooden staircase leads part of the way down a steep, bare embankment to the pools, which are located on the banks of the Lussier River in the East Kootenays in Southeastern British Columbia. Elevation 3,800 feet. Open all year.

Natural mineral water flows out at 110° into the uppermost pool, with stone edging, measuring five by three feet and three feet deep. The second pool with a gravel bottom and rock walls is twelve feet in diameter and about one and one-half feet deep. The third pool is ten feet in diameter and about two feet deep. The water in the third pool can be adjusted by diverting water from a small cold spring into the pool. A good way to cool off is to just step out of the pools and into the river. The two lowest pools, about eight feet square and one and one-half feet deep, are usually flooded out during all but the driest part of the year (watch for glass in the bottom of these pools). Water temperatures starting at 110° decrease in each pool down the line, with the lower pools registering between 100-107°. The substantial water flow keeps the water in the pools clean. The sign prohibiting nudity is very often ignored in the evening after dark.

There is a small outhouse that doubles as a changing room, and there are garbage cans in the parking area. Bring water with you. The nearest campground is about three miles east on the same road. A small store is located in Canal Flats, and the nearest gas station and lodgings are to be found in Fairmont, twenty miles north on Hwy 93.

Directions: From the village of Canal Flats, head south on Hwy 93 for three miles to a well-marked turnoff on the east side of the highway to Whiteswan Lake Provincial Park. Follow this road (Whiteswan forestry road) for 11.5 miles. The springs are well marked on the south (right) side of the road (the large sign on the north side indicates the beginning of Whiteswan Lake Provincial Park). As this road is quite busy all year round with logging trucks and mining trucks hauling ore, please drive with your headlights on.

Note: From Ram Creek, continue on same road to Lussier. Turn left at "T" and go past entrance to BC Parks. Lussier Hot Springs clearly marked on left, a total of 15 miles from Ram Creek.

Source map: *Invermere Forest District Map* (BC Forest Service). Phone: 250 342-4200.

GPS: N 50 08.148   W 115 34.542

122   MIETTE HOT SPRINGS
Jasper National Park Box 2579

780 866-3939

800 767-1611

Jasper, AB T0E 1E0

www.parkscanada.gc-ca/hotsprings

Dubbed "the hottest hot spot in the Rockies," Miette is located in a remote part of beautiful Jasper National Park with a spectacular view of Ashlar Ridge. Elevation 4,500 feet. Open May to October.

Natural mineral water flows out of several springs at temperatures up to 129° and is piped to two outdoor pools where it is treated with chlorine and maintained at approximately 103°. The first pool is shallow with a lounging area and wheelchair access. The second pool is deeper. A cold plunge was also recently added. The entire facility is designed for handicap accessibility. Bathing suits are required and can be rented, along with towels, at the facility.

Locker rooms are available on the premises. A coffee and snack bar offer picnic lunches and snacks to enjoy at the outdoor picnic area with evening barbeques available. Camping is close by at Pocahontas or accommodations can be had at Miette Bungalows. An interpretive trail leads to the hot springs source and there is much superb hiking area in subalpine mountain terrain with ample opportunity to view wildlife. It is eleven miles to all other services. Major credit cards are accepted and a valid National Park permit is required.

Directions: From the town of Jasper, drive 44 km (26 miles) east on AB 16 to Pocahontas, then turn southeast on Miette Road to the springs.

Miette circa 1935

First developed by the fur traders in the 1800s, a stone and log dam allowed cool water from a nearby creek to mix with the very hot mineral springs water. During the Depression era the original aquacourt, consisting of a concrete pool and bathhouse, was built about two miles from where the new facility is today.

123A   BANFF UPPER HOT SPRING
Banff National Park Box 900

403 762-1515

Banff, AB TlL 0C0   800 767-1611

www.parkscanada/hotsprings

Totally renovated and updated, this Parks Canada hot springs is surrounded by the beautiful scenery of Banff National Park, seventy-five miles west of Calgary. Elevation 5,176 feet. Open all year. Winter rates.

Natural mineral water at 117° flows out of a spring located fifty yards southwest of the pool entrance and is piped to a new outdoor hot pool with bench seats all around. Water temperature in the swimming pool is slightly lower than the current spring output temperature. An enlarged central island includes a children's wading area. Bathing suits are required, and suits and towels may be rented at the pool. All areas are handicap accessible with ramps into the pool.

Changing rooms with heated floors and handicap changing areas are available. A day spa with aromatic steam, aromatherapy and massage are offered by appointment. On the premises is a licensed pool-side restaurant, deck-side snack bar, a gift store, and a picnic area. A self-guided trail explains the natural history of the area. It is one mile to a store and motel and four miles to overnight camping and RV hookups. Credit cards are accepted, and a valid National Park permit is required.

Directions: Take Banff Avenue across the Bow River Bridge. Turn left, then right on Mountain Avenue. Banff Hot Springs is at the end of this road.

Courtesy of Banff National Park

Over 350,000 visitors a year. enjoy these hot waters. For fun you can even rent historic 1920s swimsuits.

123B   CAVE AND BASIN HOT SPRING
Banff National Park
Banff, AB T0L 0C0

The swimming pool was closed in 1992, and only the interpretive center is currently open.

124 MANITOU SPRINGS RESORT HOTEL AND MINERAL SPA

PO Box 967   306 946-2233
                       800 667-7672

■ Manitou Beach, SK S0K 4T0
www.manitousprings.ca

Large, new resort hotel and spa featuring indoor pools filled with mineral-rich water pumped from Little Manitou Lake, located seventy miles southeast of Saskatoon. Elevation 500 feet. Open all year.

Lake-bottom mineral springs supply the lake with water three times saltier than the ocean. This highly buoyant water is pumped to three indoor pools. The exercise pool is maintained at 94°, the soaking cove is maintained at 98°, and the water massage pool is maintained at 102°. Fully wheelchair accessible. Bathing suits required.

Hotel rooms, restaurant, bar, gift shop, retail mall, total body care services and massage are available on the premises. A service station and store are located on the corner. Credit cards accepted.

Directions: From the town of Watrous, 70 miles southeast of Saskatoon, drive three miles north on SK 365 to Manitou Beach and follow signs to the Spa.

The lake at *Manitou Springs* has a specific density similar to that of the Dead Sea, so it's impossible to sink. What a fun experience!

125   TEMPLE GARDENS MINERAL SPA

24 Fairfield St. East   306 694-5055
                                   800 718-7727

■   Moose Jaw, SK S6H 0C7
http://templegardens.sk.ca

Four-and-a-half star resort hotel and spa featuring "perfectly natural" geothermal mineral pools and suites with piped in mineral water. Pools open to the public. Open all year.

Ancient seabeds, 4,500 feet below the earth's surface, produce the natural hot mineral water which is piped to the indoor swimming pool where the temperature is kept at 100° and to the outdoor pool which is kept at 104°. The pools are treated with chlorine and hydrochloride acid in the amounts deemed necessary by local health laws. Areas of the hotel are handicap accessible. Bathing suits required.

Luxurious guestrooms include spa suites that feature two person whirlpool tubs filled with hot natural mineral water. A dining room, pool-side cafe, banquet and convention facilities, the "Oasis" spa treatment center featuring multiple types of body treatments, and a spa shop can all be found right on the premises. For spa treatments phone for reservations. Any other services can be found ten minutes away in Moose Jaw. Credit cards accepted.

The name Moose Jaw comes from the Cree Indian word "Moosegaw" meaning warm breezes. Historical tours of the town are available including tours of the Tunnels of Moose Jaw where "history goes underground."

Courtesy of Temple Gardens

WASHINGTON

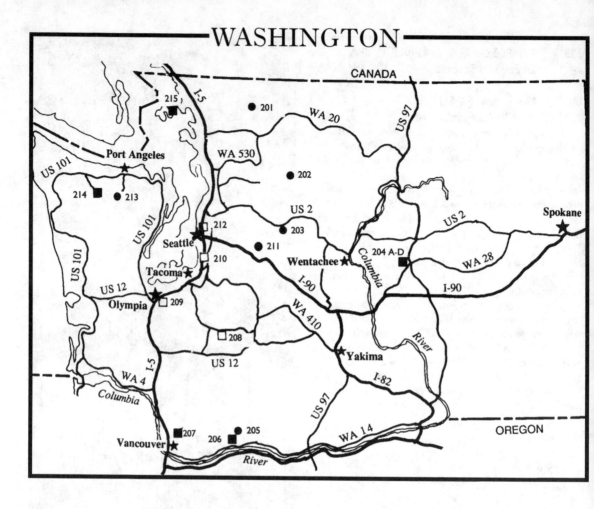

This map was designed to be used with a standard highway map.

MAP SYMBOLS

● Non-commercial mineral water pool

■ Commercial (fee) mineral water pool

□ Gas-heated tap or well water pool

〰 Paved Highway

– – – Unpaved road

⋯ Hiking road

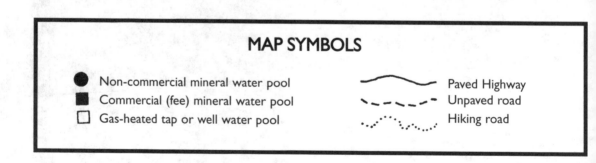

52

201   BAKER HOT SPRINGS

● **North of the town of Concrete**

Charming, primitive spring located at the end of an easy 600-yard path through the lush, green timber of Mt. Baker National Forest. Elevation 2,000 feet. Open all year; winter ski-in or snowmobile.

Natural mineral water bubbles up through vents into the bottom of a large, round, sometimes murky, sandy-bottom pool at 95-100°. Water temperature is controlled by diverting the water from a small, adjacent cold stream. Volcanic ash on the bottom of the pools sometimes clogs vents. Dig down to clear the vents and the water temperature is 102-106°. At times water will spill out through a channel to a nearby shallow "kiddie pool." The apparent local custom is clothing optional, although it is often necessary to be patient when clothed people are using the pool and are uncomfortable with nudity. Two large logs across the trail limit handicap accessibility.

There are no facilities on the premises. There is a private resort and campground located three miles away. Facilities include cabins, camping sites with hookups, boating, and a mini-store. It is thirteen miles to a telephone at Lake Tyee Campground. All other services are twenty miles away in Concrete.

Baker Hot Springs seems to attract first-time soakers and many families, especially during the summer.

Directions: From SR 20, follow Baker Lake Road for 18 miles to FS 1130, which is 0.1 miles past the bridge over Boulder Creek. In 1.5 miles, at fork, go straight toward Rainbow Falls. At the next "Y" turn right on FR 1144 for 0.5 miles to the parking turnout on left. The trail to the springs will be on the south side. This is a wider, better graded road than the logging road.

Alternate: (This road has very deep potholes). From I-5 at Burlington, five miles north of Mt. Vernon, follow SR 20 approximately 22 miles east to the Baker Lake turnoff. Turn north on Brandy Creek Road for 20 miles to Baker Lake Resort. Directly across from the resort entrance road is a logging road. Follow this unpaved, deeply rutted road for 3.2 miles to a parking turnout on both sides of the road. An unmarked, easy trail begins at the north end of the parking area on your left.

Source map: *Mt. Baker-Snoqualmie National Forest* (hot spring not shown).

GPS: N 48 45.780   W 121 40.020

307B   ECHO ROCK HOT SPRINGS
(see map on page 67)

● **Southwest of the town of Owyhee**
Northwest of Jordan Valley

Large pool and hot shower with breath-taking views along the shores of Owyhee Reservoir a few miles above Leslie Gulch and surrounded by native plants and grasses. This is a sensitive area administered by the Bureau of Reclamation. Treat it carefully. Elevation 3,000 feet. Open all year; best in the early spring if you decide to hike in or part of the trail is underwater earlier. Reached either by boat or strenuous hike.

Natural mineral water bubbles out of the ground and flows down hill to a rock-lined pool about twelve feet across and two feet deep. Water temperature varies according to the time of year. In winter the source is 108°, climbing to 115° by mid summer. The water flows out of the pool and continues down hill where it is collected in a pipe that creates a very nice shower at about 103°. Volunteers have built a large wooden platform next to the shower. Clothing optional.

Directions by boat: From Jordan Valley, take US 95 north about 18 miles to a sign directing you to Succor Creek State Park and Leslie Gulch. In about 10 miles take the left turn to Leslie Gulch and in about 15 miles you will reach the edge of Owyhee Reservoir and a boat ramp. Launch your boat and head upstream about 4 miles to where the shower and wooden platform has been built. Climb up to the pool.

Directions by hike: (Courtesy of Evie Litton) Follow above directions to boat ramp. During low water you can hike along the reservoir. At high water, join the mountain goats and walk upstream from the ramp where you'll notice a faint path that angles up a meadow, then climbs steeper slopes to disappear just above a large rocky outcrop. A very narrow path, 10 inches on average, is wider than it appears from below and is well packed. After accomplishing this short but strenuous climb, and after crossing above the first pinnacle and rounding a bend, the track continues across the face and passes above several more outcrops before finally dropping steeply to the river at Spring Creek. From here the going isn't too tough when the water level is low. Follow the long reservoir 3 miles upstream, following the bends on a map. Watch for warm water crossing your path and follow them to their source. The one-way trip is about 5 miles and is best done with a map where the spring is indicated but not named.

Source maps: USGS *Rooster Comp and Diamond Butte.*

GPS: N 43 18.120 W 117 22.980

Chuck Ensign

308   THREE FORKS HOT SPRINGS
(see map on page 67)

(see map on page 67)

●   **Southeast of the city of Rome**

Two small pools on the east side of the river and a gem of a secluded pool and waterfall on the other. Located in the upper Owyhee River Canyon, south of Jordan Valley, with spectacular sunsets visible from springs and nearby campground. Elevation 4,000 feet. Open all year; wet weather may make roads impassable, and high water makes it dangerous to ford the river.

Natural mineral water flows at 95° from several sets of springs on the east bank and winds its way through the grass toward the river and into two small pools. On the west bank, several showers cascade 95° water into a beautifully clear, gravel-bottom pool. The prevailing custom is clothing optional. The entire creek that produces the waterfalls is warm and there are dozens of soaking opportunities up the creek.

It is three miles to Three Forks, a primitive BLM campground, and fifty-one miles to all other services in Rome.

Directions: From Rome, proceed 18.2 miles east on OR 95 to milepost 36. Turn right (south) on excellent gravel road Consider this point 0. At 7.4 miles bear right, at 8.3 miles bear left, at 16.7 miles bear left, at 28.6 miles bear right, and at 31.4 miles you are on a bluff looking down into the valley. At 32.8 miles there is a "T". The campground is 2.8 miles to the right. Turn left to the springs and at 33.2 there is a wooden bridge. Cross the bridge and at 33.4 bear left at the "T". The road from here is very steep and rocky. (You may want to consider walking the remaining 2.2 miles.) At 35.4 miles there is a small, steep pullout in the rocks where 2-3 vehicles may park. Two small pools are located on the hillside below the road across from the turnout. The majority of the pools are located on the other side of the river above the waterfalls. At 35.6 miles the road ends near the river where you would cross and walk up to the springs. Trailers and motorhomes not recommended. High clearance, four-wheel drive vehicles are best.

Note: The springs are on private, unposted land. Please take particular care to leave nothing but footprints.

GPS: N 42 31.812 W 117 11.082

If you (and your vehicle) are up to it, you may have the opportunity to have a private soak in one of the many pools at the end of the trail.

Photos by Chris Andrews

Photos by Chris Andrews

309   WHITEHORSE RANCH HOT SPRING
(see map on page 67)

● **South of the town of Fields**

A very remote, primitive hot spring requiring about twenty-six miles of unpaved road travel in the dry, south-eastern corner of Oregon in the Alvord Desert. Elevation 4,000 feet. Open all year.

Natural mineral water at 114° bubbles up through the bottom of a volunteer-built, twelve-foot sandy-bottomed soaking pool that is about eighteen inches deep, crystal clear and ranges in temperature from 104-112°. The overflow runs into a second pool, three to four-feet deep, that ranges in temperature from 70-90°, depending on air temperature and wind conditions. Clothing optional.

There are no services on the premises, but there is plenty of level space on which overnight parking or tenting is not prohibited. A new concrete outhouse was built by, and the area is currently maintained by, the Oregon Dept. of Fish and Wildlife, Vale District BLM. It is forty-five miles to all services in Burns Junction.

Directions: From Burns Junction on US 95, go 21 miles south on US 95, then turn west on a mostly good gravel road and go 21 miles to Whitehorse Ranch. About 2.5 miles past the ranch, where the fence line ends, turn left on well-traveled dirt road. Drive 2.5 miles to the spring. If you miss this road, proceed approximately five miles from the ranch and turn left on a dirt road. Immediately take the left fork. Utility pole on right is B 281. Drive 2.1 miles. Bear right at old cattle loading ramp. Spring is on right, and a new concrete toilet is just past the spring on left.

Coming from Denio junction, NV, drive north on Oregon Harney County Rd 201 for 12 miles. Turn right (east) 8 miles south of Fields and continue on gravel road 29 miles, following signs to Whitehorse Ranch. Continue with above directions.

Source map: BLM *Southern Malheur*.
GPS: N 42 16.542 W 118 15.930

Photos by Skip Hill

310A BORAX LAKES HOT SPRING
(see map on page 67)

● **Northeast of the town of Fields**

In a desert area dotted with hot pools, many too hot to soak in, this last pool on the north end of the ridge finally gets us to a perfect soak in the arid Alvord Desert. Elevation 4,200 feet. The ground around the pools is ecologically fragile. Please take care. Open all year.

Natural mineral water comes up through two sources in the bottom of a large pond at 103°. The crystal clear water fills the muddy-bottom pool which is surrounded by a deposit of built-up tufa. Clothing optional.

There is plenty of level ground to camp on. Gas and limited grocery supplies can be found in Fields. The nearest large town northeast of the springs is Burns Junction, approximately fifty miles away. Come prepared with gas, water and supplies–this is the desert.

Directions: From Fields, go north about a mile plus on SR 205 continuing straight on the gravel road that has a sign saying "Highway 78, 62 miles." In 0.4 of a mile you will notice a power substation on the right with a power line road heading into the desert. Take this road, following the power lines for a few miles until the road turns left. The power line will continue, but take the well worn road through a couple of gates and pass Lower Borax Lake. After passing several more gates you will start to see the hot pools. Check the temperature of each one until you find the one that's right for you. The one at the end of the road is highly recommended.

GPS: N 42 20.167 W 118 36.163

310B ALVORD HOT SPRINGS
(see map on page 67)

● **Northeast of the town of Fields**

Funky hot springs pools, formerly a popular bathhouse, located on the vast sandy Alvord Desert area of eastern Oregon, on the east side of Steen Mountains. Elevation 4,000 feet. Open all year.

Hot 116° water with a slight sulfur smell flows out of the ground at various spots along the edge of the hill and into an algae-filled pond in a marshy grasslands along the west side of the desert. From the ponds it flows through a channel to the old bathhouse. One ten-foot by ten-foot by five-foot pool is enclosed in a roofless tin shed along with a separate dressing room. The other pool, almost as large is outdoors. Inflow can be plugged until desired soaking temperature is reached. Pools have plugs for draining and cleaning. Water continually flows through a pipe into the two algae-filled pools and runs off into the desert through a gully. Although the pools are visible from the road bathing suits are not necessary.

There are no services and no shade but plenty of level ground for overnight parking. Gas, groceries, a cafe, motel, propane and an RV park are located in Fields.

Directions: Drive north from Fields on County Rd. 201, a good gravel road, for 25 miles. You'll see the tin shed sitting all by itself in the dry desert lake bed, on the east side of the road.

GPS: N 42 32.627 W 118 31.968

For your information: McDermitt, a small town on the Oregon-Nevada border has a motel, RV park, country store with gas, and a casino run by the local tribes.

Skip Hill

311   FISHER HOT SPRING
(see map on page 67)

● **Northeast of the town of Adel**

A bathtub out in the middle of the Alvord Desert surrounded by grasses and views of the high desert mountains and plateaus within the Hart Mountain National
Antelope Refuge. Elevation 4,500 feet. Open all year.

Hundreds of gallons of 140° water flows from the
springs, but the only place to soak is an old bathtub where
you must wait for the water to cool before getting in.
Clothing optional.

There are no services available on the premises, but
there is an abundance of ground on which overnight parking is not prohibited. It is forty miles to all other services
in Adel.

Directions: Head east from Adel on OR 140. At 4.8
miles turn left and travel on this dirt road for 7.7 miles to
a fork in the road. Take the left fork and head north
toward the big flat butte and an old ranch. Continue 2.8
miles passing east of the old ranch, take the road to the
right and go 50 yards to the spring.

GPS: N 42 17.820 W 119 46.560

312 HART MOUNTAIN (ANTELOPE) HOT SPRING

(see map on page 67)

● **North of the town of Adel**

Semi-improved hot spring enclosed by a roofless, cement block wall and a larger primitive pool Surrounded by miles of barren plateau within the Hart Mountain National Antelope Refuge. Elevation 6,000 feet. Open all year.

Natural mineral water flows out of a spring at 98°. The edge of the spring has been cemented to create a soaking pool that maintains that temperature. The cement block enclosure is built to keep the animals out of the hot pool. The five-foot by ten-foot pool is approximately five-feet deep has an uneven rock bottom, and a set of stairs which makes it handicap accessible with assistance. There is no posted clothing policy, which leaves it up to the mutual consent of those present. A sign says "Nude bathers must lock door." (No one does.)

Fifty yards west of the block building is another source at almost 106°. A six-foot pool, about one and one-half feet deep has been dug out of grasses and offers an amazing view.

There are no services available on the premises, but there is an abundance of ground on which overnight parking is not prohibited. It is twenty miles to a cafe and store and forty miles to all other services in Adel. There is also a small general store with a gas pump in the town of Plush. Hart Mt. Headquarters visitors room is open twenty-four hours for maps, brochures, wilderness permits.

Directions: At the north end of the town of Plush is a small sign directing you to turn right to get to Hart Mtn Refuge, 23 miles. This is Lake County Rd. 3-12 which starts out paved but after 13 miles turns to gravel. Once you enter the refuge, and just past the Headquarters, there is a sign directing you to the springs and campground, 4 miles away.

Note: The last seven miles of gravel road is very steep. Carry plenty of water for you and your vehicle.

Source map: *Hart Mountain National Antelope Refuge*

GPS: N 42 30.060 W 119 41.580

Photos by Idaho Dippers

The enclosure that contains the cement pool was built to keep out the animals. However, if you don't mind sharing, there is this natural pool available.

Courtesy of Summer Lake

313 SOUTH HARNEY LAKE HOT SPRINGS
(see map on page 67)

● South of Burns Junction

Pool located at the south end of Harney Lake in an area called the Harney Basin surrounded by a large meadow area dotted with lakes and thermal water. Elevation 4,200 feet. Open all year.

Natural mineral water with a great flow meanders down through the grasses in a small channel and is diverted into two pools. The upper pool is too hot to soak in. The water cools from 109° as it fills the lower pool which is about ten feet around and two to three-feet deep. The pool might be handicap accessible with assistance. Bathing suits would be handy on busy weekends.

There is plenty of level ground and places for camping. All services are 34 miles away in Burns.

Directions: From Burns head south on OR 205. 0.9 miles south of mile marker 23 turn west onto South Harney Road. Continue west 8.2 miles to the fork and bear right. The springs are 0.2 of a mile further on.

Source map: Oregon Geothermal (HA 64).

GPS: N 43 10.812 W 119 03.456

Summer Lake is listed in the Historic Register as the oldest spa-related structure in Lake County. This area is of particular interest to wildlife/bird enthusiasts. Big-horn sheep can be viewed through binoculars from the premises and possibly from these new outdoor tubs. The Summer Lake Wildlife Refuge, several miles north on Highway 31, is a nesting area for many species of birds.

314 SUMMER LAKE HOT SPRINGS
541 943-3931

■ Paisley, OR 97636   877 492-8554

www.summerlakehotsprings.com

Indoor pool in the wide-open spaces south of Summer Lake located off Hwy 31 which has just been designated a National Scenic Highway. Elevation 4,200 feet. Open all year.

Natural mineral water flows out of a spring at 110° and cools as it is piped to the pool building. Water temperature in the fifteen by thirty-foot indoor pool is maintained at 102° in the winter and 100° in the summer on a continuous flow-through basis that requires no chemical treatment of the water. Bathing suits required.

A two bedroom ranch-style home with its own outdoor soaking pool can be rented. Dressing rooms, overnight camping, and RV hookups are available on the premises. Buildings are heated geothermally. Vintage trailers are available for overnight accommodations. It is six miles to all other services. No credit cards accepted.

Future improvements will include outdoor pools, and more cabins. Call for status.

Location: Six miles northwest of the town of Paisley on OR 31. Watch for sign on north side of road at mile marker 92.

Chris Andrews

Photos by Phil Wilcox

315 LITHIA SPRINGS INN

■ 2165 W. Jackson Rd.   800 482-7128
Ashland, OR 97520
www.ashlandinn.com

Built in the country tradition, Lithia Springs Inn, just outside of the charming town of Ashland, is located on a unique geographical wonder—a natural hot spring.

An artesian well pumps hot natural mineral water at 100° into the inn where it is used to fill the in-room whirlpool tubs and provide much of the heating. The water temperature is boosted, and most of the sulphur smell is removed from the water.

Besides providing all of the luxurious amenities found at this up-scale Bed and Breakfast, including a bountiful breakfast, you can also order a massage in your room. Small conference facilities available. Major credit cards accepted.

It is only two miles to the center of Ashland. Phone for reservations and directions.

Sharing a private soak in one of the two person tubs surrounded by an artistically decorated room.

316 JACKSON WELLSPRINGS

■ 2253 Hwy 99 N.   503 482-3776
Ashland, OR 97520

Jackson WellSprings is in the process of building a sanctuary for mind, body, and spirit. Elevation 1,650 feet. Open all year.

Natural mineral water flows out of three springs at 100-115° and directly into an outdoor swimming pool that maintains a temperature of 87°. A very large water flow allows for cleaning twice a week. (Chlorine is only used on extremely crowded days.) There are two indoor soaking tubs, one individual tub with jets, and one large enough for two persons, in which heated natural mineral water can be controlled up to 110°. These tubs are drained and cleaned after each use so that no chemical treatment of the water is necessary. There is ramp access to the pool house with assistance available upon request. Bathing suits are required, except in private soaking rooms. Clothing optional time may be after dark.

Locker rooms, picnic and play area, patio area in a garden setting, full RV hookups and tent and tepee sites, swimming lessons, water aerobics, Watsu Therapy, a sauna, and professional massages are available on the premises. Summer musical events are presented and parties can be arranged for. All other services are a few miles away in Ashland. Expansion plans include large gardens with medicinal and edible plants, a modern clinic, and varying therapy programs. Credit cards accepted.

Location: Two miles north of Ashland at the Valley View Road exit from US 99.

317   UMPQUA HOT SPRINGS
(see map)

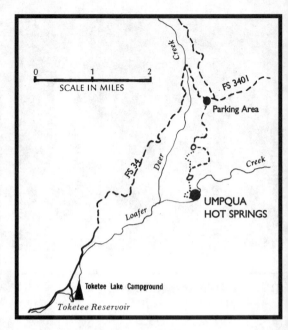

Phil Wilcox

● **Northwest of Crater Lake**

Popular, semi-improved hot spring on a wooded bluff overlooking the North Umpqua River, in the Umpqua National Forest. Elevation 2,600 feet. Open all year.

Natural mineral water flows out of a spring at 108° and is carried by hose directly into a sheltered, six-foot by six-foot pool that volunteers have carved out of the spring-built travertine deposit. The only way to cool the water in the tub is to remove the hose. There is also a very hot upper tub, around 112. Two other volunteer-built rock pools are slightly down hill and somewhat cooler. There are no posted clothing requirements, and the location is quite remote, so a clothing-optional custom would be expected. However, the location is so popular, especially on summer weekends, that it is advisable to take a bathing suit with you. You may have to wait your turn to share a rather crowded pool.

There's an outhouse at the springs and a restroom/changing room at the parking lot. It is three miles to a Forest Service campground and twenty-five miles to all other services.

Directions: Drive 60 miles east of Roseburg on OR 138 to Toketee Junction. Turn north on paved road FS 34 (Toketee Rigdon Road). Drive 2.3 miles, turn right on FS 3401 (Thorn Prairie Road), and drive 2 miles to the parking area. Walk across the bridge over the North Umpqua River, bear right on the North Umpqua Trail, and climb 1,200 feet east to springs. The first third of the trail is quite steep.

Source map: *Umpqua National Forest.*

GPS: N 43 17.796 W 122 21.834

Linda Nabon

Besides providing year-round protection from weather extremes, the shelter helps keep the ubiquitous mosquito away.

Bob Seal

318   MCCREDIE HOT SPRINGS

● **East of the town of Oakridge**

Easily accessible, primitive hot springs with a strong skinny-dipping tradition, located on the north and south banks of Salt Creek in the Willamette National Forest. Elevation 2,100 feet. Open all year; day use only.

Natural mineral water flows out of several springs on the north bank at 120° and on the south bank at 140°. The water is channeled into a series of shallow, volunteer-built, rock-and-mud pools where it cools as it flows toward the creek. The pools on the south bank tend to be larger and around 100°. There are hot jets on the bottom of the creek, so be careful. Despite the proximity of a main highway, the apparent local custom is clothing optional.

There are no services available on the premises. A large, level parking area permits parking from sunrise to sunset only. It is less than one mile to a Forest Service campground and ten miles to all other services.

Directions: To reach the springs and pools on the north bank drive from the town of Oakridge, drive approximately 10 miles east on OR 58 past Blue Pool Campground. At 0.1 miles past mile marker 45, turn right (south) into a large parking area between the road and the creek. Walk to the upstream (east) end of the parking area and follow a well-worn path 40 yards to the springs.

To reach the springs and soaking pools on the south bank, drive 0.5 miles east on OR 58, turn right on Shady Gap Road across the bridge, and stay right on FS 5875. Drive 0.1 miles, park, and look for an overgrown path that follows the creek 0.25 miles back downstream to the pools.

GPS: N 43 42.342 W 122 17.292

Photos by Phil Wilcox

The short distance from the trailhead makes this an ideal place to bring your family and introduce children to the joys of hot springs.

319   MEDITATION POOL (WALL CREEK) WARM SPRING

● **Northeast of the town of Oakridge**

Idyllic, primitive warm spring on the wooded banks of Wall Creek at the end of a short, easy trail in the Willamette National Forest. Elevation 2,200 feet. Open all year for day use only.

Natural mineral water flows up through the gravel bottom of a volunteer-built, rock-and-sand pool at 104°. The pool temperature ranges up to 96° depending on air temperature and wind conditions. While the water is not hot enough for therapy soaking, it is ideal for effortless lolling. The apparent local custom is clothing optional.

There are no services available on the premises. It is five miles from the trailhead to a Forest Service campground and nine miles to all other services.

Directions: In Oakridge turn north off OR 58 at stop light. Go over railroad track and turn east (right) onto First St. which becomes FS 24. Nine miles from firehouse, turn (left) north on FS 1934 (sign says "Blair Lake 8 miles") for 0.5 miles on gravel road and watch for trailhead sign on (left) west side of the road. There is no name or number given for the trail at the trailhead area. Follow a well-worn path along Wall Creek for 600 yards to the creekside pool. Tree sign says "Warm Springs Trail No. 3582."

Source map: *Willamette National Forest.*
GPS: N 43 48.438   W 122 18.690

Photos by Phil Wilcox

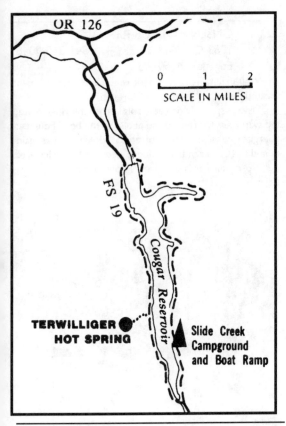

Linda Nabon

Directions: From OR 126 approximately five miles east of Blue River, turn south on FS 19 along the west side of Cougar Reservoir. The marked hot-springs trailhead is on the west side of the road just past milepost 7 and 0.3 miles south of Boone Creek. A large parking area is on the east side of the road, 0.1 miles beyond the trailhead. Parking is permitted from sunrise to sunset only.

Reference map: *Willamette National Forest* (hot springs not shown).

GPS: N 44 05.004 W 122 14.328

320 TERWILLIGER (COUGAR) HOT SPRINGS

(see map)

● **Southeast of the town of Blue River**

A lovely series of user-friendly, log-and-stone soaking pools in a picturesque forest canyon at the end of an easy quarter-mile trail in the Willamette National Forest. Elevation 3,000 feet. Open all year for day use only. Small permit fee.

Natural mineral water flows out of a spring at 116° and directly into the first of a series of four volunteer-built log and rock pools, each of which is a few degrees cooler than the one above. A log across one of the pools creates a small waterfall. Water temperature may vary depending on flow. An organized group of volunteers has also built access steps and railings. The apparent local custom is clothing optional.

There are no services available on the premises except for a pit toilet. There is a walk-in campground within 0.5 miles. Overnight parking is prohibited along the road for one mile on both sides of the trailhead. It is four miles to a Forest Service campground and eight miles to all other services.

Skip Hill

322   ONSEN HOT TUB RENTALS
❏   1883 Garden Have.   541 345-9048
      Eugene, OR 97403

Well-maintained, enclosed, rent-a-tub establishment located near the University of Oregon.

Private-space hydrojet pools using chlorine-treated tap water are for rent to the public by the hour. Fourteen fiberglass tubs in open-roof enclosed spaces are maintained at 102°. Each unit includes a covered dressing area.

No credit cards accepted. Phone for rates, reservations, and directions.

321   SPRINGFIELD SPAS
❏   1100 Main St.   503 741-1777
      Springfield, OR 97477

Well-maintained, suburban, rent-a-tub establishment located on the main street in downtown Springfield.

Private-space hydrojet pools using chlorine-treated tap water are for rent to the public by the hour. Twelve fiberglass tubs in open-roof enclosed spaces are maintained at 102°. Each unit includes a covered dressing area with shower and stereo. Handicap accessible.

Four tanning beds are available on the premises. Credit cards accepted. Phone for rates, reservations, and directions.

Photos by Jayson Loam

Phil Wilcox

323 BELKNAP RESORT AND HOT SPRINGS
59296 Belknap Springs Rd.
541 822-3512

■ **McKenzie Bridge, OR 97413**

Riverside resort, newly remodeled, and with very attractive grounds, in a wilderness setting surrounded by the lush greenery of Willamette National Forest. Elevation 1,700 feet. Open all year.

Natural mineral water flows out of a spring at 196° and is piped into a combination reservoir and heat exchanger where heat is extracted for space heating and for the hot water supply in the lodge and the RV park. The cooled mineral water is piped to outdoor pools at the lodge and the RV park. Both pools are lightly treated with chlorine and maintained at a temperature of 100-102° in the winter and 100° in the summer. Four lodge rooms have indoor hydrojet tubs controllable up to 110°. The pools are available to the public as well as to registered guests. Bathing suits required.

Six cabins, eighteen lodge rooms, fifteen tent and forty-two RV hookup sites, and snack bar are available on the premises. Arrangements can be made for fishing and white water rafting. It is six miles to all other services. Credit cards accepted. Phone for reservations.

Location: On OR 126, six miles east of the town of McKenzie Bridge. Follow signs.

A steel bridge takes you across the river to the spring's source and the many hiking trails through the surrounding forest.

Chris Andrews

Bob Seal

324   BIGELOW (DEER CREEK) HOT SPRING

● **Northeast of the town of McKenzie Bridge**

A small, rock-and-sand pool in a fern-lined grotto on the McKenzie River. Elevation 2,000 feet. Open all year.

A small flow of natural mineral water (130°) bubbles up from the bottom of a volunteer-dug pool, maintaining a comfortable 102-104° soaking temperature. The apparent local custom is clothing optional.

There are no services available on the premises. It is 1.5 miles to a campground (Ollalie), three miles to a motel and RV hookups (Belknap Hot Springs), and six miles to all other services.

Directions: From the town of McKenzie Bridge, drive nine miles northeast on OR 126. Drive 0.4 miles past milepost 15, then turn left onto FS 2654 (Deer Creek Road). Park just beyond the bridge over the McKenzie River. Follow the signed McKenzie River Trail at the down stream side of the bridge and immediately take the lower trail for the short hike to the pools.

GPS: N 44 14.460   W 122 03.480

Whoever has jurisdiction here at the springs has mandated that the springs are only to be open from sunrise to sunset. A hefty fine ensues for those caught using the spring after dark. While this may seem harsh, it is often the only way that the springs can be protected from those who wish to use it as a "party spot," and do not haul away their trash, and generally abuse the spring. This rule is certainly better than closing the spring altogether. Please cooperate so that the spring may remain open.

Linda Nabon

325 KAH-NEE-TA RESORT
PO Box 120, 6823 Hwy 8 503 553-1112
Warm Springs, OR 97761

Oregon's only destination resort with Casino excitement, Spa Wanapine, an eighteen hole golf course, and a variety of lodging options, all owned and operated by the Confederated Tribes of Warm Springs. In these foothills on the east side of the Cascade Mountains, the sun shines 300 days a year. Elevation 1,500 feet. Open all year.

Natural mineral water flows out of a spring from the Warm Spring River at 140° and is covered as it is piped into the hot springs pool, where it is cooled to a pleasant 95°. Pools are treated with chlorine. The lodge pool is unheated. The hot spring pool is available to the public as well as to registered guests. Many areas are handicap accessible. Bathing suits are required.

Spa Wanapine, the European style beauty spa features a variety of massage, and body treatments, pedicure and manicures, facials and waxing. Hydrotherapy tubs, and a sauna and steambath are also available.

The resort is host to the fine dining experience of the Juniper Rooms, a gourmet buffet in the Chinook Room, and three snack bars are located at the village, golf course and casino. Activities include a championship eighteen-hole golf course, miniature golf, kayaking, trail rides on horseback, hiking, biking, tennis, volleyball, and basketball, and a casino. The lodge boasts 139 refurbished rooms. The village offers thirty-one rooms and Tee Pee camping spaces. Full RV hook-ups are available in the village area. It is eleven miles to a store and service station. All major credit cards accepted.

Directions: From US 26 in Warm Springs, follow signs 11 miles northeast to resort.

Kah-Nee-Ta caters to 5,000 guest per day at this fully equipped resort that can provide space for a huge convention or offer a night's stay in a tepee. The focal point of the 600,000-acre reservation is the Museum at Warm Springs —Oregon's first Native American museum.

326 BREITENBUSH HOT SPRINGS RETREAT AND CONFERENCE CENTER

PO Box 578   503 854-3314

■ Detroit, OR 97342

This rustic retreat has been renovated by the intentional community that operates it as a worker-owned cooperative. The resort is located on the banks of the Breitenbush River, surrounded by the Willamette National Forest. Elevation 2,300 feet. Open all year; periodically closed camps.

Natural mineral water flows out of springs and artesian wells at temperatures up to 180°. Four covered outdoor soaking tubs use flow-through mineral water requiring no chemical treatment. Each is maintained at a different temperature ranging from 60-111°. Three outdoor pools in a sacred meadow overlooking the river operate on a flow-through basis with temperatures averaging between 100-110°, depending on weather conditions. The sauna house sits atop a 180° mineral spring. Tubs and pools are available to the public for day use as well as to overnight guests, but prior reservations are strongly advised. Clothing is optional in the tubs and sauna area unless a workshop leader requests special swimsuit-required times.

Massage, hydrotherapy, and aromatherapy, as well as vegetarian meals, and cabins are available on the premises. Daily well-being programs such as yoga and ecstatic dance, are offered without charge.

It is eleven miles to a store, service station and phone, one and one-half miles to overnight camping, and seventy miles to RV hookups. Organizations and individuals are invited to request rates for facilities suitable for seminars and conferences. Visa and MasterCard are accepted.

Location: Eleven miles northeast of Detroit. Phone for rates, reservations, and directions.

Whether you attend an educational healing seminar or a mushroom hunt, *Breitenbush Hot Springs* with its access to the river—and several tubs to view it from—offers an ideal place to relax and enjoy nature.

Courtesy of Breitenbush Hot Springs

Besides the springs by the river, there are several other spiritual and relaxing places to soak.

327   BAGBY HOT SPRINGS

●   Southeast of the town of Estacada

One of the best: a well-planned rustic facility featuring hot mineral water supplied through a 150-foot log flume. A lush rain forest and tumbling mountain stream make the 1.5 mile access trail enjoyable in its own right. Elevation 2,200 feet. Open all year.

Natural mineral water emerges from two springs at 135° and is flumed to an outdoor, round cedar tub on a deck at the upper spring site (102°)and to two bathhouse buildings at the lower springs. The partially-roofed bathhouse is a replica of the one that burned down in 1979 and offers five hand-hewn cedar tubs in private rooms. The open-sided bathhouse offers a single communal space containing three hewn tubs and a round cedar tub. A flume diversion gate at each tub brings in more hot water whenever desired. The temperature in the individual tubs ranges from 98-108°. All tubs are drained and cleaned daily so no chemical treatment of the water is necessary. There are no posted clothing requirements, and the apparent custom in the communal bathhouse is clothing optional.

A Forest Service employee is at the springs Wednesday through Sunday. There is a picnic area on the premises, but no overnight camping is permitted. A walk-in campground is located at Shower Creek, one-third of a mile beyond Bagby. A drive-in Forest Service Campground (Nohorn) is located adjacent to the trailhead parking area, and the Pegleg Falls Campground is located one-half mile northeast of the trailhead. All other services are available thirty-two miles away in Estacada.

Directions: From Estacada head south on OR 224 about 40 miles to the junction with OR 63. Continue on SR 63 to FSR 70. Drive about 10 miles on OR 70 to the Bagby Hot Spring Trail Head and parking area. When you are almost at the springs the trail will split; take the left fork over the bridge. The trail into Bagby has been widened and topped with a cement-like coating.

GPS: N 44 56.160 W 122 10.380

A network of wood flumes and pipes carries the hot water to the individually controlled tubs in the bathhouse—a replica of the one that burned down in the 1970s. The half roof seems to be slanted in such a way as to keep the sun off in summer and the snow away in winter. The walk in through an absolutely gorgeous forest and along fern-lined streams only adds to the anticipated pleasure of a delightful soak.

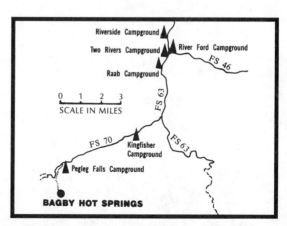

328 FOUR SEASONS HOT TUBBING

19059 SE Division   503 666-3411

❑   Gresham, OR 97030

Attractive, suburban rent-a-tub facility featuring enclosed outdoor tubs. Open all year.

Private-space hot pools using chlorine-treated tap water are for rent to the public by the hour. The six enclosed, outdoor fiberglass hydrojet pools are maintained at a temperature of 104°. Each unit includes indoor dressing room, shower, and toilet.

Visa and MasterCard are accepted. Phone for rates, reservations, and directions.

Phil Wilcox

Jayson Loam

329 OPEN AIR HOT TUBBING

11126 NE Halsey   503 257-8191

❑   Portland, OR 97220

www.cgwc.org

Unique, suburban rent-a-tub featuring open-roofed wood patios. Open all year.

Private-space hot pools using chlorine-treated tap water are for rent to the public by the hour. Six enclosed outdoor fiberglass hydrojet pools are maintained at temperatures ranging from 102-104°. Each unit has an outdoor water spray over the pool and an indoor dressing room with shower and toilet. Three of the units can be combined to accommodate a party of twenty-four. There is a sauna in one unit. Handicap accessible (no pool ramps).

AM/FM cassettes, cable television, VCR in one room and a sauna are available for use. Credit cards accepted. Phone for rates, reservations, and directions.

330   INNER CITY HOT TUBS, COMMON GROUND WELLNESS CENTER

❏ 2927 NE Everett   503 238-1065
Portland, OR 97232
www.cgwc.org

Open-air, family-style pools and sauna in a garden setting near downtown Portland. This non-profit community corporation offers classes in health and relaxation.

Two communal hydrojet pools, cool tub, sun deck, steam room and flotation tank are for rent to the local community and public by the hour. Both hot pools use gas-heated tap water and are maintained at 104°. Bathing suits are optional in the pool and sauna areas.

Hakomi therapy, counseling, yoga, Thai and Shiatsu massage, breath and energy work, spinal care, acupuncture and Chinese herbs, natural vision classes, and more are available on the premises. Credit cards accepted. Phone for rates, reservations, and directions.

Photos by Phil Wilcox

331   PORTLAND TUB AND TAN

❏ 8028 SE Stark St.   503 261-1180
Portland , OR 97215
www.PortlandTubandTan.com

Downtown facility with hi-tech, computerized water chemistry located in the commercial district off the Stark St. exit from the 205 freeway. Open all year.

Four tubs in private, air-conditioned rooms offer computerized water chemistry for your safety, a restroom, shower and towels in each room, and DMX stereo for your enjoyment. The tubs are completely sanitized after each use and the water is chlorinated. Tub temperatures vary between 103-104°.

A Wolff tanning system and massage by appointment are offered on the premises. Credit cards accepted. Phone for rates, reservations, and directions.

Portland Tub and Tan

332   ELITE HOT TUBBING AND MASSAGE THERAPY

4240 SW 10th   503 641-7727
Reservations 503 641-7735
❏ Beaverton, OR 97005

Private rent-a-tub suites conveniently located off of Hwy 217. Open all year.

Private-space hot pools using chlorine-treated tap water are for rent to the public by the hour. Six indoor fiberglass hydrojet pools are maintained at a temperature of 103°. Each suite includes a shower, sink, toilet and radio.

Singles and couple massage is available on the premises and they will help you put together a massage and tubbing package for that special occasion. Visa and MasterCard accepted. Phone for rates, reservations, and directions.

Kathee Scott

Chris Andrews

421 SALMON HOT SPRING
248 Hot Springs Rd.   208 756-4449
■ Salmon, ID 83467

Rustic rural plunge with a colorful past and history dating back over 100 years, currently undergoing major renovation while remaining open to the public on a day-use fee basis. Elevation 4,950 feet. Open all year.

Natural mineral water flows abundantly out of a spring at a temperature of 113° and is piped to a fifty-foot outdoor recreational swimming pool that is maintained at 98° to 102°. The eighteen-foot soaking pool is maintained at 104°. Other pools are available for overnight guests only. The flow-through pools are drained and refilled nightly, so no chemical treatment of the water is needed. Bathing suits required.

Dressing rooms and snacks are available on the premises. Ample level ground is available for tent camping and self-contained RVs. It is eight miles to all other services in Salmon. Credit cards are accepted.

Directions: From Salmon, drive 4.5 miles south on US 93, turn left on Airport Road to a "T" intersection. Turn left again and follow Warm Springs Creek Road 3 miles to the spring.

422 SHARKEY HOT SPRING
● East of Salmon

Two new cement pools built by the Bureau of Land Management in an open sagebrush canyon above the Lemhi Valley. Elevation 5,300 feet. Open all year.

Natural mineral water flows out of a spring at 105° directly into the two new pools. The pools are fenced off to keep out the animals. The apparent local custom is clothing optional.

There is also a new dressing room area, tables and fire pit. No camping is allowed. It is twenty-three miles to all services.

Directions: From Salmon, drive east on ID 28 to the Tendoy store. Turn left, go 0.2 miles and turn left again on Tendoy Lane. Drive 2.8 miles and turn right onto Warm Springs Wood Road. Follow this dirt road for 1.9 miles to the high voltage power line. Park in the parking area and walk to the spring.

Source map: *Salmon National Forest.*
GPS: N 45 00.630 W 113 36.708

423   GOLDBUG HOT SPRINGS

● **Southeast of the town of Salmon**

Many delightful pools and cascades of various temperatures at the end of a steep, two-mile trail up a beautiful canyon in Salmon National Forest. Elevation 5,200 feet. Open all year.

Natural mineral water flows out of several springs at temperatures up to 100° and combines with cold creek water as it tumbles down the canyon. Volunteers have added rock-and-sand dams to deepen the water-worn cascade pools. Temperatures in these cascade pools are determined by the rate of cold water runoff. Some of the pools offer a spectacular view down the canyon. The apparent local custom is clothing optional although the area is very popular and you may need to negotiate.

There are no services available on the premises. Parking is available at the trailhead, and it is one mile to all other services in Elk Bend.

Directions: On US 93 approximately 23 miles south of Salmon, look for mile marker 282. Go east on a short gravel road to the trailhead parking area. This parking lot is adjacent to private property. Cross the footbridge over Warm Springs Creek and follow the often steep trail up the canyon to the springs near the top of the ridge.

GPS: N 44 54.318   W 113 55.776

These two gentlemen are visitors from the United Kingdom. What a great new experience for them as there are no hot springs where you can soak in the UK.

Photos by Chris Andrews

Chris Andrews

Bob Sea

Sally Jackson (pictured above) is not only a visitor from New Zealand, but she writes hot springs books about all the wonderful places to soak there.

Soakers are attracted to both the warm water and the multitude of tropical fish that swim around.

424   CRONKS CANYON HOT SPRINGS

● **North of the town of Challis**

Small soaking tub situated in a high rock-wall canyon on the bank of the Salmon River just twenty feet from US 93. Elevation 4,700 feet. Open all year.

Natural mineral water flows directly into this seven by ten-foot pool, just big enough for two to soak comfortably. The low flow of the 115° water generally keeps the water at a good soaking temperature. A bucket is handy for adding river water on hot days. Clothing optional, although keep a suit near by. Due to the steep bank the pool is not visible from the highway.

There are no services available on the premises, and the nearest campground, Cottonwood, is five miles to the south. You can buy a drink and mail a letter in Ellis, about two miles away; otherwise all other services are about twenty miles to the south in Challis.

Directions: Take US 93 north out of the small town of Ellis about three miles to mile marker 266.6. (It is 2 miles from the general store.) There is a small parking area capable of holding a couple of cars about 250 yards upstream of the spring which is on the west side of the road.

Source map: USGS *Challis*, 15 min.
GPS: N 44 43.140 W 114 00.996

425   BARNEY HOT SPRINGS

● **Northeast of the town of Challis**

A large warm pond located in a remote and scenic valley (BLM land) in the middle of the high desert, with a magnificent view of two mountain ranges. Elevation 6,400 feet. Open all year; road not maintained in winter.

Natural mineral water flows into the pond from a spring at one end of the pool. The 83° water fills the very large, four-foot-deep pond. The pool is visible from the road, so bathing suits are advisable.

There are no services available on the premises. It is one-half mile to Summit Creek Campground and sixty-five miles to all other services in Challis.

Directions: From Challis, drive north on Hwy 93 for 17 miles to Ellis. Turn east toward May and Patterson on the Pahsimeroi Road. Follow this road about 25 miles past Patterson to Summit Creek Campground. The pool is 0.5 miles past the campground on the opposite side of the road.

Source maps: USGS *Gilmore*; *Challis National Forest* (East).
GPS: N 44 16.146 W 113 27.036

426 CHALLIS HOT SPRINGS
H/C 63 Box 1779   208 879-4442
■ Challis, ID 83226

Historic pools, turn-of-the-century boardinghouse, and campground on the banks of the Salmon River. A wonderful place to observe bighorn sheep and golden eagles and enjoy outdoor activities. Elevation 5,000 feet. Pools open all year; campground open April 1 to November.

Natural mineral water from several artesian springs at temperatures up to 127° bubbles up directly into the indoor and outdoor pools that require no chemical treatment. The temperature of the outdoor pool is maintained at approximately 90°, and the temperature of the indoor pool ranges from 104-110°. Easy to get around for people who need assistance. Bathing suits are required.

A six room bed and breakfast, changing rooms, snacks, picnic areas, camping and RV hookups (dump station) are available on the premises, along with hiking, bird watching, cycling, and a driving range. It is eight miles to all other services in Challis. Major credit cards accepted.

Directions: From the intersection of US 93 and ID 75 near Challis, go southeast on US 93 and watch for signs to the hot springs which is 4.5 miles off of US 93.

Photos by Chris Andrews

427 WARM SPRINGS CREEK

● **Northwest of the town of Dubois**

Two nice rock-and-sand pools in the desert foothills south of the Beaverhead Mountains, best appreciated in the hot summer as water is on the cool side. Elevation 6,400 feet. Open all year; last three and one-half miles of road not maintained year around.

Natural mineral water at 84° flows directly into two pools. The first pool is fairly shallow and large enough for two to three people. The second pool is much deeper and will hold six to eight people comfortably. Clothing optional but keep a swimsuit handy.

There are no facilities on the premises but there is a lot of level space where overnight camping is not prohibited. There is a small swimming hole located at the camping area at the 10.7 mile mark. All other services are thirty miles away in Dubois.

Directions: From Dubois (exit 167 on I 15) travel west on ID 22 17.9 miles. Turn north on a road marked "Warm Springs. Crooked Creek" and continue 7.9 miles to a fork in the road. Take the right fork towards Warm Springs Creek. Continue past several camping areas until you reach a cattleguard at 11.4 miles. Immediately past the cattleguard turn right and travel 0.1 mile to the fenced spring area.

Source map: USGS *Edie Ranch*.
GPS: N 44 15.198 W 112 38.442

Courtesy of Heise Hot Springs

428 GREEN CANYON HOT SPRINGS
Box 235   **208 458-4454**
■ **Newdale, ID 83436**

Chris Andrews

Rural, indoor plunge and RV park in a really green canyon. Elevation 6,000 feet. Open every day except Sunday from April to the end of September; open weekends the rest of the year.

Natural mineral water flows out of a spring at 118° and is piped to pools and a geothermal greenhouse. The indoor swimming pool is maintained at 96°, and the outdoor hydrojet pool is maintained at 105°. No chemical treatment is necessary. Bathing suits are required.

Locker rooms, snack bar, picnic area, streamside campground and RV hookups are available on the premises. Used extensively for family reunions and church group gatherings. It is twenty-one miles to all other services. No credit cards are accepted.

Directions: From the town of Driggs, go north and west 17 miles on ID 33. At Canyon Creek bridge, turn south and follow signs four miles to the resort.

429 HEISE HOT SPRINGS
5116 E. Heise Rd.   **208 538-7312**
                                     800 828-3984
■ **Ririe, ID 83443**

Modernized, family-oriented resort, priding itself on home-away-from-home hospitality, with spacious, tree-shaded picnic areas and RV sites. Located on the north bank of the Snake River. Elevation 5,000 feet. Open all year; closed November.

Natural mineral water flows out of a spring at 126° and is piped to an enclosed hydrojet pool that is maintained at 105° and requires some chemical treatment. Tap water, treated with chlorine and heated by geothermal heat exchangers, is used in the other pools. An outdoor soaking pool is maintained at 92-93°, the large swimming pool at 82°, and the waterslide pick-up pool at 85°. Bathing suits are required in all areas.

Locker rooms, pizza parlor, convenience store, tackle shop, overnight camping, RV hookups, picnic area, and golf course are available on the premises. Some of the world's finest cutthroat trout fishing is nearby. It is five miles to all other services. No credit cards are accepted.

Directions: From the town of Idaho Falls, go east 22 miles on US 26 and then follow signs four miles north across the river to the resort.

The only advantage to a drought year is that the pool at Alpine Warm Springs is available for a soak.

430   ALPINE WARM SPRINGS

● **Southwest of Alpine, WY**

Single, large pool located on a flat area on the south edge of Palisades Reservoir, one-hundred feet down from the high water mark. Elevation 5,600 feet. Only accessible very late in the season when the reservoir is low or during years with very little rainfall.

Natural mineral water bubbles up from the bottom into an eight by twelve-foot oval pool dug out of the earth at a comfortably warm 105°. Clothing optional.

McCoy Creek campground is three-quarters of a mile away at the trailhead and all other services are twelve miles away in Alpine.

Directions: Beginning at Alpine Junction in Alpine, Wyoming travel south on US 89 approximately 4 miles to McCoy Creek Rd. (FR 087). Turn right (west) and drive about 6 miles to the bridge over McCoy Creek. Park here and follow the edge of the reservoir approximately 0.75 miles north to the spring.

Source map: USGS Alpine, 7.5 minute (springs not shown).

GPS: N 43 12.102 W 111 06.444

> Note: This hot springs is included in both the Idaho and Wyoming sections. You must go into Wyoming to get there although the spring is actually in Idaho.

Photos by Chris Andrews

If you don't mind a challenging hike, this might be the perfect hot springs—no problem with skinny dipping up here, and hardly ever crowded.

431 BEAR CREEK HOT SPRINGS

● **Southwest of the town of Palisades**

Large rock-and-sand pool near the head of a beautiful canyon in the Caribou National Forest at the end of a strenuous seven mile hike. Elevation 6,900 feet. Creeks are not safe to wade across during spring run-off; wait until mid-summer. Consider spending the night.

Natural mineral water at 98° seeps up through the bottom into a large (10 by 20 feet) rock-and-sand pool, over two-feet deep, and capable of holding a dozen people. There are other small pools to soak in at the outflow of the large pool where the warm water forms a stream running through the grass. Clothing optional.

There are no facilities on the site, however there is plenty of open ground to camp on. It is approximately seven miles to Bear Creek campground and eleven miles to all other services in Palisades.

Directions: From the town of Palisades drive southeast on US 26 towards Alpine Way. Turn right 3.1 miles and drive across the dam. Bear left 1.6 miles later at the fork onto FS 058 (towards Bear Creek campground). Drive 5.6 miles on FS 058 and turn right into the campground. Continue 0.3 of a mile to the end of the road and the trail head. **The hike:** From Bear Creek campground follow trail up Bear Creek. The trail roughly follows the creek. It will be necessary to ford several side streams on the way or take alternate routes up the steep bank that roughly parallels the main trail to keep your feet dry. At about 4 miles you will have to cross the North Fork of

Bear Creek and continue walking up the trail along the main fork of Bear Creek. Approximately 6 miles up the trail you will cross to the south side of the creek. In about 200 yards, it intersects the Big Elk Mountain Trail (148) heading up a very steep ridge. Watch closely for this junction—the trail sign is often missing. Turn left and head up Big Elk Mountain Trail. Follow Trail 148 heading southeast up a very steep ridge, gaining nearly 900 feet in under 1 mile. When the trail flattens out at the crest watch for a trail that bears off to the left. This 0.6 mile little trail (not marked on any map) winds down and up, down and up, then down once more to an unofficial camping area and the spring. The spring is a total of 1.5 miles off the main Bear Creek Trail.

Source maps: *Caribou National Forest*, USGS *Red Ridge, Idaho* (springs not on maps).

GPS: N 43 16.098 W 111 18.246. (This would be the time to buy a GPS navigator.)

432A LAVA HOT SPRINGS FOUNDATION

430 East Main   800 423-8597
Lava Hot Springs, ID 83246
www.lavahotsprings.com

Two attractive and well-maintained recreation areas operated by a self-supporting state agency in the town of Lava Hot Springs. Elevation 5,000 feet.

GEOTHERMAL POOLS: (East end of town; open 363 days per year.) Natural sulphur-free mineral water flows out of the ground at 112° and directly up through the gravel bottoms of a Roman-style pool in a sunken garden and of a large, partly shaded soaking pool. No chemical treatment is necessary. Pool temperatures range as low as 107° at the drain end of the soaking pool. The same water is pumped to two partly shaded hydrojet pools where cold shower water may be added to control the pool temperature. Handicap accessible. Bathing suits required. Massage is available on the premises.

SWIMMING POOLS: (West end of town; open Memorial Day through Labor Day; weekends in September.) Hot mineral water is used to heat the Olympic Swimming Complex to a comfortable 90°. Hydroslide tubes and diving platforms round out the exciting visit. Bathing suits required.

Locker rooms are available at both locations, and it is less than three blocks to all other services. Visa and MasterCard accepted, no personal checks. (See following listings for accommodations.)

Photos by Chris Andrews

Courtesy of Riverside Inn

432B RIVERSIDE INN

255 Portneuf Ave. 208 776-5504

Outside Idaho 800 733-5504

■ Lava Hot Springs, ID 83246

A faithfully restored historic hotel built originally in 1914, once known as the Elegant Grand Inn, picturesquely situated on the banks of the Portneuf River in an area noted for skiing, fishing, and hunting. Close to summer and winter recreation. Elevation 5,400 feet. Open all year.

Natural mineral water is pumped out of a well at 133°, then piped to two small, and one large indoor private soaking pool and one outdoor soaking pool overlooking the river where the water has now cooled down to 104°. Pools operate on a continuous flow-through basis; no chemical treatment of the water is needed. The pools are available to the public as well as to registered guests. Not handicap accessible. Bathing suits required in public areas.

Sixteen nonsmoking rooms and suites, twelve with a private bath, are available on the premises. A restaurant featuring fine dining and lounges for smoking and non-smoking are available. Hotel space is heated with geothermal water. All other services are within three blocks. Major credit cards accepted. Phone for rates and information.

432C HOME HOTEL AND MOTEL
TUMBLING WATERS MOTEL

306 E. Main 208 776-5507

■ Lava Hot Springs, ID 83246

www.homemotel.com

Home Hotel, recently remodeled featuring hot mineral baths with jetted tubs in twenty-two of the twenty-six units, and in their rental house. There are also two outdoor tubs with a view of the surrounding mountains. Situated between the two Lava Hot Springs Foundation locations (see previous page).

Tumbling Waters Motel is across the street from the public hot pools and is located right next to the river. Two complimentary passes given for each week-night's stay for use in the public hot pools. All rooms at both locations are non smoking.

It is less than three blocks to a cafe, store, service station, overnight camping, and RV hookups. Credit cards accepted. Be sure to phone for reservations.

Courtesy of Home Hotel

432D LAVA HOT SPRINGS INN BED AND BREAKFAST

94 E. Portneuf Ave.

208 776-5830
800 527-5830

Lava Hot Springs, ID 83246
www.lavahotspringsinn.com

This beautifully restored historic building in downtown Lava Hot Springs was originally built in 1925 as the Lava City Sanitorium and Hospital and later served as the Valley View Rest Home. Elevation 4,500 feet. Open all year; pools also available to the public for a small fee.

The water is supplied by geothermal wells at 145° and is piped to several soaking pools with temperatures ranging from 105-112°. No chemical treatment is necessary. There is also a four foot deep twenty by eighty foot therapy pool at about 90°and a small cold plunge.

The resort offers twenty-three rooms, nine of which have large jetted tubs and individual bathroom facilities. The other rooms are nestled in the wings of the building with ample shared baths. Family suites are also available. The pools and breakfast are included in the room rate for registered guests and the pools are available to the general public for a small fee. Call for midweek room and soak specials. Bring along a bathing suit, though you may not need it midweek depending on the crowd. All areas are non-smoking. Spa facilities are coming soon. All credit cards accepted.

Located just east of the Lava Hot Springs Foundation Olympic Pool complex. Pilots, land at the restricted landing strip in Lava Hot Springs and call for a pick up. It is just a few blocks to all services.

Photos by Chris Andrews

Chris Andrews

Courtesy of Riverdale Resort

433A RIVERDALE RESORT
3696 N. 1600 E.   **208 852-0266**
Preston, ID 83263

New commercial development in a rural valley subdivision. Elevation 4,000 feet. Open all year.

Natural mineral water is pumped from a geothermal well at 120°, then piped to various outdoor pools. All soaking pools are flow-through and drained daily, eliminating the need for chemical treatment of the water. The partly shaded hydrojet pool is maintained at 103-105°, and a large soaking pool is maintained at 97-100° in the summer and 102-104° in the winter. The chlorinated junior Olympic swimming pool is maintained at 86° in the summer. Two chlorinated waterslide catch pools are maintained at approximately 80°. Handicap accessible. Bathing suits are required.

A new eight-unit bed and breakfast with whirlpool tubs is a recent addition to the modern hotel rooms, all of which are non-smoking rooms. Locker rooms, snack bar, three camping areas, RV hookups (eighteen with water and power) and an RV dump station are available on the premises. It is less than six miles to a cafe, store, service station, and motel. Credit cards accepted.

Directions: From Preston on US 91, go six miles north on ID 34 and watch for the resort signs.

433B MAPLE GROVE HOT SPRINGS
11386 N Oneida Narrows Rd.
     208 851-1137
Thatcher, ID 83283
www.maplegrovehotsprings.com

This delightful recently renovated small resort is located in a valley along the Oneida Narrows Reservoir. It originally operated as a commercial hot springs from the early 1900's until the 1960's.

Multiple springs feed one large "source" pond averaging 130° which is then piped to the therapeutic soaking pools. The pools operate on a flow-through basis, so no chemical treatment is necessary. Temperatures are adjusted seasonally and range from 92-103° summer and 100-108° winter. There are three areas to soak in: one very large thirty-five by forty foot soaking pool, and two beautiful round rock and mortar soaking pools. These large pools can comfortably seat a couple of dozen soakers each, and offer the best view on the property, overlooking the scenic reservoir. Bathing suits required.

On site services include showers and lavatories, locker rooms, and a community kitchen. A few snacks and conveniences are also for sale. Several "rustic" campsites can be rented nightly and reservations are accepted for groups or individual sites. All services are available in Grace, about sixteen miles away.

Directions: Beginning in the town of Grace Idaho, drive south approximately 13 miles on ID 34 to mile marker 29.1. Just before crossing the Bear River turn left on 13800 North Rd, then immediately turn right on to Maple Grove Rd. Follow Maple Grove Rd approximately 3.1 miles to a Y, then bear right 0.2 miles to the resort. Boaters are always welcome to motor up the reservoir to the resort, park on the bank, and walk to the office.

Check their website for current rates and other information.

Located near the old Oregon trail, Indian Springs was the winter camp ground for the Shoshoni Indians.

Plan to stay at our bed and breakfast or campground and enjoy the swimming pool, ride the breathtaking Black Hole or Dragon Water Slides, splash in our newly added water playground or just soak in our large hot tub.

434   DOWNATA HOT SPRINGS
25901 Downata Rd.   208 897-5736
■ **Downey, ID 83234**
www.downatahotsprings.com

Expanded, older, rural pool and picnic grounds in the rolling hills of southeastern Idaho. Elevation 4,000 feet. Call for open days and hours.

Natural odor and taste free mineral water flows out of a spring at 112° and is piped to outdoor pools treated with chlorine. The main swimming pool and the waterslide catch pool are maintained at 85-95°, and a hot tub, minimally chlorinated is maintained at 104-106°. A new 105° water slide and two new hydrotubes are the latest additions. Bathing suits required.

Bed and breakfast, campground, tepee rentals, snack bar, dressing rooms, picnic areas, lighted volleyball court, basketball and baseball facilities are all available on the premises. Holiday parties and arthritis classes available during the off peak season. Most areas at the resort are handicap accessible. It is three miles to a store, service stations, and a motel.

Directions: Take Downey exit off I 15 to US 91. Drive 3 miles south of the town of Downey and watch for signs.

435   INDIAN SPRINGS RESORT
3249 Indian Springs Rd.   208 226-2174
■ **American Falls, ID 83211**

Cottonwoods, willows and Russian olive trees shade the new, large hot tubs and pool in a rural Idaho setting where birds and animal life are abundant. Elevation 4,500 feet. Open all year.

Natural mineral water flows out of a spring at 90° and is piped to an Olympic size outdoor swimming pool that is treated with a minimum of chlorine and maintains a constant temperature of 90°, which it has for over a century. The pool is gravity fed and the water moves through the pool every five and one-half hours, rather than being filtered and recirculated. Two large hot tubs under the trees that can hold up to 150 people is kept at 104-106°. Some areas are handicap accessible. Bathing suits required.

Locker rooms, picnic area, tent sites, and 125 full-hookup RV spaces are available on the premises. Cabins are in the process of being built. Call for status of construction. It is three miles to all other services. Credit cards are accepted.

Location: Take exit #36 (ID 37) south off of I 86. Continue 1.8 miles on ID 37 to resort.

Nat-Soo-Pah is an Indian name meaning "Magic Mineral Water."

436 NAT-SOO-PAH HOT SPRINGS
2738 E. 2400 N. 208 655-4337
■ Hollister, ID 83301

One of the cleanest and quietest facilities of its kind, with soaking pools and acres of tree-shaded grass for picnics and overnight camping. Located on the Snake River plain, south of Twin Falls. Elevation 4,400 feet. Open May 1 to September 15.

Natural mineral water flows out of a spring at 99° and is piped to three outdoor pools. The swimming pool, maintained at 92-94°, uses flow-through and chlorine treatment. The twenty-five person soaking pool is maintained at a temperature of 104-106°. The hydrojet pool, supplied by direct flow-through from the spring, maintains a temperature of 99° and requires no chemical treatment. There is also a ninety foot waterslide at the side of the swimming pool. Bathing suits are required.

Locker rooms, snack bar, picnic area, forty-six overnight camping spots, and twenty-nine full RV hookups are available on the premises. It is four miles to a store and service station and 16 miles to a motel. No credit cards accepted.

Directions: From US 93, 0.5 miles south of Hollister and 0.5 miles north of the Port of Entry, go east three miles on Nat-Soo-Pah Road directly to the location.

Photos by Chris Andrews

437   DESERT HOT SPRINGS
208 857-2233

■   Rogerson, ID 83302

Funky western-style pool, bathhouse, bar, and RV park in need of some repair in a remote section of the Jarbridge River Canyon. Elevation 5,100 feet. Open all year.

Natural mineral water flows out of two springs at 129° into an outdoor, chlorine-treated cement tub and two indoor, flow-through soaking pools that require no chemicals. The outdoor pool is maintained at temperatures ranging from 80-90°. The three smaller, two-person tubs are maintained at 104° and 107°. Pools are open to the public in addition to registered guests. Bathing suits are required in the pool and public areas.

Dressing rooms, cafe, gas pump, cabins, overnight camping, and RV hookups are located on the premises. Horseback rides available. It is forty-nine miles to a store and service station. No credit cards are accepted.

Directions: From Twin Falls, go approximately 27 miles south on US 93. Watch for a highway sign and turn southwest 0.5 miles into Rogerson. At the main intersection, watch for Desert Hot Springs* highway sign and follow signs 49 miles to the location. Only the last two miles are on gravel road.

*The signs in Rogerson and along the way still call it Murphy Hot Springs.

Phil Wilcox

438A   BANBURY HOT SPRINGS
PO Box 348   208 543-4098
■   Buhl, ID 83316

Community plunge on the Snake River with soaking pools and a spacious, tree-shaded area for picnics and overnight camping. Elevation 3,000 feet. Open mid-May to Labor Day.

Natural mineral water flows out of a spring at 141° and is piped to a large, outdoor, chlorine-treated pool that is maintained at a temperature of 89-95°. Mineral water is also piped to five private-space soaking pools, some equipped with hydrojets. Water temperature in each pool is individually controlled. Each soaking pool is drained, cleaned, and refilled after each use, so that no chemical treatment of the water is needed. Bathing suits are required except in private-space pools.

Locker rooms, snack bar, overnight camping, RV hookups, and a boat ramp and dock are located on the premises. It is four miles to a restaurant and twelve miles to a store, service station, and motel. No credit cards are accepted.

Directions: From the town of Buhl, go 10 miles north on US 30. Watch for the sign and turn east 1.5 miles to the resort.

Chris Andrews

Debbie Johnson

438B   MIRACLE HOT SPRINGS
■   19073A Hwy 30   208 543-6002
    Buhl, ID 83316
    www.mhsprings.com

Beautifully remodeled to include private pools, and geodesic domes for overnight stays and large group events. Surrounded by rolling agricultural land. Elevation 3,000 feet. Open all year including holidays; closed Sundays.

Natural mineral water flows out of a well at 139° and into a large outdoor swimming pool kept at 95-100° in the winter and cooler in the summer. The hotter soaking pool is maintained at temperatures from 105-110°. Both pools operate on a flow-through basis requiring no chemical treatment and are drained and cleaned nightly. Fifteen very nicely appointed regular, and four VIP suites, each have their own private tub where you can control the temperature. Hydraulic lifts have been installed in the two outdoor pools. Bathing suits are required in public areas. All buildings and dressing rooms are geothermally heated.

Six geodesic domes provide a unique environment for retreats, workshops, etc. In addition one of the domes complete with palm trees and grass year round, shaded and screened during the summer, can be used by all as a picnic area. Camping domes furnished with sleeping pads can hold up to six people, a larger dome, up to ten people, and the dome suite, furnished with a queen bed, is handicap accessible. RV hookups and camping sites are located along the Salmon Falls Creek. Therapeutic massage is offered. A restaurant is available within three miles, and all other services are available within ten miles. No credit cards accepted.

A place to relax, for any reason, in any season. The geodesic domes provide places to stay and a place for group seminars. The private pools are very nicely done, and their special "romance package" certainly sounds inviting.

Location: On US 30, ten miles north of the town of Buhl and nine miles south of the town of Hagerman.

Phil Wilcox

Chris Andrews

439 SLIGAR'S THOUSAND SPRINGS RESORT

18734 Highway 30   208 837-4987
Hagerman, ID 83332

Indoor plunge with private-space hydrojet tubs and green, shaded RV park with a view of multiple waterfalls on cliffs across the Snake River. Elevation 2,900 feet. Open all year.

Natural mineral water flows out of a spring at 200° and is piped to an indoor swimming pool, seventeen indoor hydrojet pools each large enough for eight people, and one indoor hydrojet pool large enough for twenty people. The temperature in the swimming pool is maintained between 90-96°, while the temperature in the hydrojet pools is individually controllable. All the pools are chlorinated. Handicap accessible. Bathing suits are required in public areas.

Locker rooms, boat dock, shaded picnic area, overnight camping, and RV hookups are available on the premises. A restaurant is within one mile, and all other services are within five miles. No credit cards accepted.

Location: On US 30, five miles south of the town of Hagerman.

While in the area treat yourself to a delightful boat ride on the Snake River to see the waterfalls up close, or better yet include a sunset dinner or a five-course Sunday brunch. For reservations and daily schedules call: 1000 Springs Tour, 208-837-9006. The river guides offer interesting historical information about the area. Tours leave the dock adjacent to Sligar's.

440 INDIAN HOT SPRINGS

East of the town of Grasmere

Rolling hills, sage brush and deep river canyons surround this soaking box located on a hillside in the high desert. Elevation 3,800 feet. Open all year; heavily rutted roads; 4 WD recommended. Be aware of washouts during rainy season.

Natural mineral water is piped to a six by six, eighteen inch deep plastic soaking box. The water starts out at 158° and cools as it runs to the pool. Several rock-and-sand pools are seasonally gouged out along the river. A very large hot water fall is nearby in a deep rocky canyon. Bathing suits not necessary.

Gas and a convenience store are located approximately seventy miles away in Bruneau. Unofficial camping is permitted at or near the springs. Whenever traveling in the desert be sure to carry sufficient supplies.

Directions: A GPS and a good map are essential for this one. Spring is located about 0.75 miles downstream of the junction of the Bruneau and Jarbridge Rivers. Actually it is on the Bruneau River. Some roads to this springs are extremely rocky. A narrow, high clearance vehicle is required and be sure your spare is in good condition.

GPS: N 42 19.980 W 115 39.000

Chris Andrews

441   LOWER INDIAN BATHTUB HOT SPRINGS

● **Southeast of the town of Bruneau**

A large soaking pool in a sheltered cove along the Bruneau River surrounded by rolling hills, sage brush and deep river canyons in the high desert. Elevation 2,800 feet. Open all year; heavily rutted roads; 4 WD recommended. Be aware of washouts during rainy season.

A large flow of natural mineral water comes up through the bottom of a large fifteen by thirty gravel bottom soaking pool at 102°. The pool is about two feet deep and is located below a cliff to protect it from the desert winds. The local custom seems to be clothing optional.

Gas and a convenience store are located eleven miles away in Bruneau. Unofficial camping is permitted at or near the springs. Whenever traveling in the desert be sure to carry sufficient supplies.

Directions: Travel southeast out of Bruneau on Hot Springs Road approximately 7.5 miles. Drive 0.7 miles and turn right (west) at the sign that says Bruneau River. Continue west for about 0.5 miles on this road which is also signed as CCC Road, then turn left staying on the Bruneau River Road. Follow this road for 0.3 miles and take the right hand fork. Follow this road for 0.7 miles. This road follows the bottom of a small narrow canyon which is too rough for a 2-wheel drive. Continue straight toward the river to the parking area about 50 yards to the east. From the parking area walk to the left side of the cliff and follow the trail about 75 yards to the springs.

GPS: N 42 46.020 W 115 43.500

442   PRINCE ALBERT HOT SPRING

● **Northeast of the town of Bruneau**

Situated on the side of the sagebrush covered Mt. Bennet Hills overlooking the entire Mountain Home Valley. Open all year.

Hot mineral water bubbles up out of the ground at 112° and runs down the hill to two soaking pools. The upper rock and dirt pool is about four feet by five feet and one and one-half feet deep with temperatures registering around 108°. A little further down hill is the slightly larger second pool (a large trough) which can be drained and only registers 102°. Bring a shovel and some bug spray. Clothing optional.

All services are back in Glenns Ferry. Unofficial camping is permitted at or near the springs. Whenever traveling in the desert be sure to carry sufficient supplies.

Directions: Take I 84 south from Boise to exit 120 at Glenns Ferry. Pass north under the freeway and take an immediate left on a paved road. Take this road 4 miles to a fork labeled Bennet Mountain Road. Turn right at the junction and go 6.6 miles. Take the well-traveled gravel road to the left 2.8 miles at which point you will take the fork on your right. After 1.5 miles and just after passing under some power lines, take the fork to your left which will take you the remaining 1.4 miles to the springs. This last stretch of road has been deeply carved and has a stream running through it. A high-clearance vehicle is not only suggested, but required. There are two jeep trails that go towards the spring on your right. Take the first one and you can park within 50 feet of the spring.

Photos by Wally Deitrich

443   WILD ROSE HOT SPRINGS

● **East of the town of Carey**

Beautiful, remote, peaceful soaking pool of crystal clear water. An abundance of wild roses near this rock and gravel pool give it its name. The area is surrounded by lava flows to the south and sparsely covered hills to the north. Elevation 5,000 feet. Open all year.

A natural mineral water spring flows over marshy ground at 100° to an 8 by 15-foot pool, up to three-feet deep and made of lava rock with a gravel bottom. The flow-through rate is rapid enough to eliminate most algae and leaves. The springs are located on BLM land, but the pool is on private land. Please use, but don't abuse. Bathing suits may be advisable as pool is close to the road. However, traffic is sparse and pool is not in sight—just don't stand up on the deck.

There are no services on the premises. It is fifteen and one-half miles to a campground at Craters of the Moon National Monument and thirty-four miles to all other services in Arco.

Directions: From Carey, drive 10 miles east on Highway 20-26-93. One-half mile east of mile marker 214, look for a small turnout on the north side of the road. Park and follow the trail north toward the hill. It's about 100 yards to the pool.

Map Sources: BLM *Craters of the Moon*; USGS *Paddleford Flat*.

GPS: N 43 21.876 W 113 47.346

Meeting new people and sharing information about the hot springs in the area is part of the fun of going to hot springs.

You get your choice between a stock tank which is a bit deeper and a natural rock pool which is fairly shallow. The view is the same.

---

444   MAGIC RESERVOIR HOT SPRINGS

● **East of the town of Fairfield**

A small soaking pool on the shore of Magic Reservoir near the boat ramp with views of the surrounding sagebrush-covered hills. Elevation 4,500 feet. Open all year.

Natural mineral water flows out of a spring which is located on private property. The water which comes out at 160° flows down a small channel to the shore of the reservoir into a small two-person rock-and-sand pool about one to one and one-half feet deep. The temperature in the pool ranges from 102-106° and can be adjusted by diverting the flow of hot water or adding cold water from the reservoir. Volunteers have also added a stock tank with hoses from the hot and cold sources to control the temperature. Handicap accessible with some assistance. Bathing suits are definitely recommended at this very public place.

There are no facilities on the premises. A store and fuel are twenty-one miles away in Fairfield.

Directions: From Fairfield drive east on US 20. Four-tenths of a mile east of mile marker 172 turn right (south) toward the Hot Springs boat landing. Continue south for 0.75 miles to the west edge of the parking area and walk approximately 75 yards to the spring.

Map Sources: BLM *Fairfield* (spring not on map); USGS: *Bellvue*.

GPS: N 43 19.638 W 114 24.000

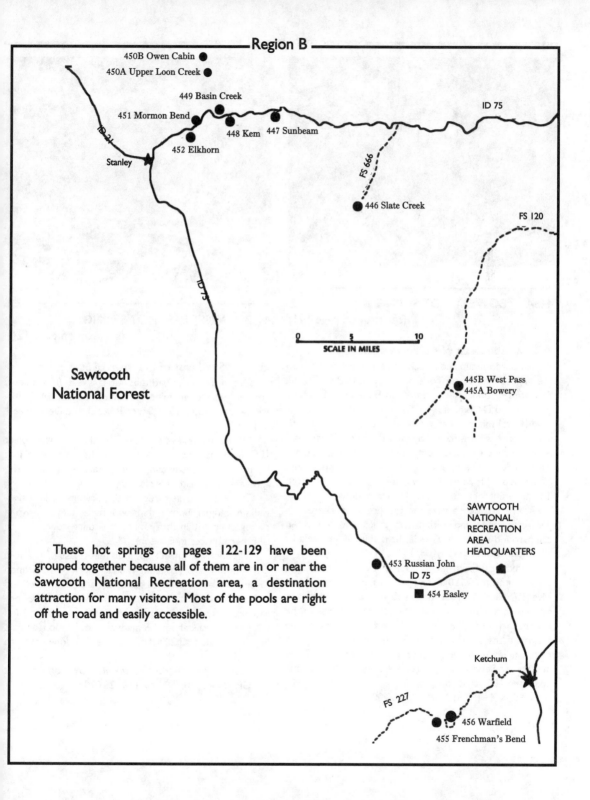

450B Owen Cabin

450A Upper Loon Creek

449 Basin Creek

451 Mormon Bend

448 Kem

447 Sunbeam

452 Elkhorn

ID 21

Stanley

FS 666

446 Slate Creek

ID 75

FS 120

ID 75

Sawtooth
National Forest

0   5   10
SCALE IN MILES

445B West Pass
445A Bowery

SAWTOOTH
NATIONAL
RECREATION
AREA
HEADQUARTERS

These hot springs on pages 122-129 have been grouped together because all of them are in or near the Sawtooth National Recreation area, a destination attraction for many visitors. Most of the pools are right off the road and easily accessible.

453 Russian John
ID 75

454 Easley

Ketchum

FS 227

456 Warfield

455 Frenchman's Bend

Chris Andrews

Bob Seal

445A   BOWERY HOT SPRING

(see map on page 121)

● **Southeast of the town of Stanley**

An outdoor tub and a rock-and-sand soaking pool on the edge of the South Fork of the Salmon River in the Sawtooth National Recreation Area. Elevation 6,800 feet. Road closed December 1 to May 1.

Natural mineral water flows out of a spring at 125° and through a hose to the tub and the pool. Water temperature in the tub is controlled by diverting the hot water inflow. Water temperature in the volunteer-built primitive pool is controlled by admitting cold river water. The apparent local custom is clothing optional.

There are no services on the premises. There is a walk-in campground within two miles and a drive-in campground within thirty miles. It is thirty-four miles to all other services in Clayton.

Directions: From ID 75, four miles east of Clayton, drive south on FS 120 along the East Fork of the Salmon River 27 miles to a gate which you will need to open, and make sure to close. Drive another couple of miles to the parking area on your left and walk upstream to the springs. If the gate is locked, you will need to hike less than 2 miles south down the service road toward Bowery Forest Service Station. At the bridge, follow a trail upstream 100 yards to the spring.

GPS: N 43 58.518 W 114 30.006

445B   WEST PASS HOT SPRING

(see map on page 121)

● **Southeast of the town of Stanley**

Out-in-the-open bathtubs along West Pass Creek, near an abandoned mine in Sawtooth National Recreation Area. Elevation 7,000 feet. Road closed December 1 to May 1.

Natural mineral water flows out of a grassy hillside at 105° and runs continuously through a hose to the ancient bathtubs, which maintain a temperature of 102°. The apparent local custom is clothing optional.

There are no services on the premises. There is a walk-in campground within two miles and a drive-in campground within thirty miles. It is thirty-four miles to all other services in Clayton.

Directions: From ID 75, four miles east of Clayton, drive south on FS 120 along the East Fork of the Salmon River 28 miles to a locked gate. Park along the fence and walk along the east side of the fence which denotes private property. (Do not go onto the private property.) You will need to walk about 1.5 miles to the abandoned mine. Hike down the trail 20 yards past the abandoned mine to the springs.

Source map: *Sawtooth National Recreation Area.*
GPS: N 43 58.860 W 114 29.070

Photos by Chris Andrews

It is still a good idea to check with the ranger as to local road and weather conditions as the road to Slate Creek was destroyed by flash floods in September of 1998 and the springs were buried under the debris that was carried down the canyon by the rushing water. There are still problems with flooding.

The historical bathhouse has recently been restored, complete with interpretive signs telling a bit about the springs.

446 SLATE CREEK HOT SPRING
(see map on page 121)

● **Southeast of the town of Stanley**

A wooden soaking box and two rock-and-sand pools in a wooded canyon in the Sawtooth National Recreation Area. Elevation 7,000 feet. Open all year.

Natural mineral water flows out of a spring at 122° and through a hose to the box, which is all that remains of a bathhouse that once stood near the HooDoo mine. Another hose brings cold water, permitting complete control of the water temperature in the box. A wooden ledge inside the soaking box lets you sit down and enjoy the soak at any temperature you'd like. There are also primitive pools on the edge of the creek. The water has a slight sulphur smell. The apparent local custom is clothing optional.

There are no services available on the premises. It is seventeen miles to gas and a convenience store and thirty miles to all other services.

Directions: Drive 24.5 miles east of Stanley on ID 75. Turn right on FS 666 (Slate Creek Road) and just over the Salmon River bridge turn south on a dirt road about 7.4 miles until the road ends. Walk in the last 0.25 mile. Wear good shoes as the landslide area is rocky and slippery.

Source map: *Sawtooth National Recreation Area.*
GPS: N 44 10.320 W 114 37.452

447 SUNBEAM HOT SPRINGS
(see map on page 121)

● **East of the town of Stanley**

Several rock-and-sand pools lining the edge of the Salmon River in Challis National Forest. Elevation 6,000 feet. Open all year.

Natural mineral water flows out of several springs on the north side of the road at temperatures up to 160°. The water flows under the road to several volunteer-built rock pools along the north bank of the river (upstream from the parking lot), where hot and cold water mix in a variety of temperatures. The path to the toilet and down to the springs would be wheelchair accessible requiring only three or four steps to the pools. As all pools are easily visible from the road, bathing suits are advisable.

A new toilet large enough to use as a changing room has recently been built and, except for the campgrounds, there are no other services on the premises. It is seven miles to all other services.

Location: On ID 75, at mile post 201, one mile west of Sunbeam Resort, northeast of the town of Stanley.
GPS: N 44 16.056 W 114 44.988

Photos by Chris Andrews

450B   OWEN CABIN HOT SPRING
(see map on page 121)

● **East of the town of Stanley**

Small pool in a large meadow near the ruins of the old Owen Cabin in a remote forested area noted for its cluster of hot springs. Elevation 5,200 feet. Open season depends on snow levels.

Natural mineral water flows out of the source spring at 120°, across the ground and into a small rock-and-gravel pool. The temperature in the pool depends a lot on air temperature, so test this one carefully before going in. Clothing optional.

There are no services on the premises, although there are spaces for pack-in camping. Tin Cup, the nearest campground, is eight miles away and all other services are 40 miles back in Stanley.

Directions: From Stanley, drive east on ID 75 13 miles to Sunbeam. Follow FS 013 north about seven miles and bear left on FS 172. Follow FS 172 over Loon Creek Summit to the Loon Creek Ranger Station. Turn right on FS 007 and follow it to the end of the road and the trailhead. Tin Cup campground is less than a mile from the end of the road. The easy hike to the springs is about 6 miles each way, approximately 0.7 of a mile past the pools at Upper Loon Creek. The road is poor and not recommended for motor homes or large trailers.

Source Maps: *Challis National Forest* (West); USGS *Rock Creek.*

GPS: N 44 39.036 W 114 44.136

451   MORMON BEND HOT SPRINGS
(see map on page 121)

● **East of the town of Stanley**

Small rock-and-sand pool on the south side of the Salmon River located in a scenic valley near several campgrounds and other hot springs. Elevation 5,600 feet. Accessible only during the summer when the river flow is low.

Natural mineral water flows out of a spring at 100° and fills a small, shallow rock-and-sand pool on the edge of the river. The pool needs to be rebuilt each year. Bring a suit, as pool is visible from the road.

Mormon Bend campground is on the north bank of the river and all other services are eight miles back in Stanley.

Directions: From Stanley drive east on ID 75 to mile marker 196.3 where a small, two-car turnout is located. A trail will lead to the river where you will then cross the river to the springs located near the inside corner of the river bend. You can also start the trail at the east end of the campground.

Source Maps: USGS *East Basin Creek; Challis National Forest* (spring not shown on either one).

GPS: N 44 15.612 W 114 50.358

Chris Andrews

452 ELKHORN (BOAT BOX) HOT SPRING

(see map on page 121)

● **East of the town of Stanley**

Small, wood soaking box perched on a rock between the road and the Salmon River in the Sawtooth National Recreation Area. Elevation 6,100 feet. Open all year.

Natural mineral water flows out of a spring at 136° and is piped under the road to a soaking box where the temperature is regulated by diverting the flow of hot water and pouring in buckets of cold river water. The box is too hot to get into without adding the cold water. Volunteer-built rock-and-sand pools beneath the box offer a very comfortable soak. Bathing suits are advisable as the location is visible from the road.

It is one mile to the Salmon River Campground and two miles to all other services.

Directions: On ID 75, 0.7 of a mile east of mile post marker 192, watch for a small turnout on the river side of the road. Walk down path toward the river.

Source map: *Sawtooth National Recreation Area* (hot springs not shown).

GPS: N 44 14.688 W 114 53.160

Phil Wilcox

453 RUSSIAN JOHN HOT SPRING

(see map on page 121)

● **North of the town of Ketchum**

Remains of an old sheepherder's soaking pool on a slope 200 yards above the highway in Sawtooth National Recreation Area. Elevation 6,900 feet. Open all year.

Natural mineral water flows out of a spring at 89° and directly into a small, clay-bottom pool that has recently been strengthened with some cement work and maintains a temperature of no more than 86°. Despite the cool temperature, this pool is so popular you may have to wait your turn. The apparent local custom is clothing optional.

There are no services available on the premises. It is eighteen miles to all services.

Directions: On ID 75, 30 yards south of mile marker 146, turn west and then south to the parking area. The trailhead is at the "Road Closed" sign and the pool is within 100 yards.

Source map: *Sawtooth National Recreation Area.*
GPS: N 43 48.402 W 114 35.256

A spectacular view for all seasons.

Bob Seal

454   EASLEY HOT SPRINGS

208 726-7522
(see map on page 121)

■   North of the town of Ketchum

Community pools located in the scenic Sawtooth National Recreation Area with an outstanding view of the Boulder Mountains, Elevation 6,800 feet. Open daily (except Mondays) in the summer and on weekends in the winter.

Hot mineral water from their own spring is gravity fed to two large outdoor soaking pools and a full size swimming pool. The soaking pools operate on a flow through basis and the swimming pool uses a minimum amount of chemicals. There is also an indoor eight-person tub with jets. Bathing suits required.

There is a convenience store on the premises and hiking, biking, and fishing are also available. Easley Campground, with limited RV spaces available during the summer, is located one mile away. All other services are fourteen miles away in Ketchum. This area is extremely popular for cross-country skiing, particularly with the famous Sun Valley Ski Resort only sixteen miles away.

Directions: From downtown Ketchum drive north on ID 75 14 miles to mile marker 142.4. Turn left and drive a few hundred yards to the resort.

455   FRENCHMAN'S BEND HOT SPRING

(see map on page 121)

●   Southwest of the town of Ketchum

Several primitive roadside pools along both banks of Warm Springs Creek. Elevation 6,400 feet. Open all year for day use only (closed 10 PM to 4 AM). Ski in during the winter.

Natural mineral water flows from the ground at more than 120° and into volunteer-built rock-and-sand pools where it is mixed with cold creek water to produce a comfortable soaking temperature. Nudity, alcohol, glass containers, non-biodegradable soap or shampoo and littering are prohibited. No constructing or altering of the pools is allowed. Rules are strictly enforced.

There are no services on the premises. Roadside parking limitations must be observed. It is eleven miles to all services.

Directions: From ID 75 (Main Street) in Ketchum, drive 10.7 miles west on Warm Springs Road. Park in the well-marked parking area and walk 200 yards upstream to the spring.

Source Map: *Sawtooth National Recreation Area.*
GPS: N 43 38.472 W 114 29.454

Photos by Chris Andrews

456 WARFIELD HOT SPRING
(see map on page 121)

● West of the town of Ketchum

Pools along the river are legal to soak in below the high water mark, although a new home has been built which blocks the old access. Elevation 6,400 feet. Open all year; dangerous during high water.

Natural mineral water seeps out of the earth at 119°, flows across the ground and into two rock-and-sand pools, one seven by ten-feet and the other fifteen by twenty-five feet. Temperatures in the pools range from 100-106°. A three and one-half foot concrete pool holds a temperature of about 110°. There are several more pools one hundred yards downstream. Diverting the cold water from the creek is the best way to regulate the water temperature in the pools. The pools often may need to be rebuilt as this spring receives little use since the house was built. As the pools are at least partially visible from the road it is a good idea to keep a suit handy.

Directions: During low water times, park in the area for Frenchman's Bend and walk up the river being careful to stay below the high water mark which is the boundary between private and public land. This is dangerous during high water, but as long as you stay below the high water mark, wading whenever necessary, there should be no problem.

Source Maps: *Sawtooth National Forest.* USGS: *Griffin Butte.*

GPS: N 43 38.394 W 114 29.232

457 WORSWICK HOT SPRINGS

● East of the town of Featherville

Dozens of primitive springs send a large flow of geothermal water tumbling down several acres of rolling hillside in the Sawtooth National Forest. Elevation 6,400 feet. Open all year.

Natural mineral water flows out of many springs at temperatures of more than 150°, supplying a series of volunteer-built, rock-and-log pools in the drainage channels. The water cools as it flows downhill, so the lower the pool, the lower the temperature. Most pools are quite shallow. The most popular pool is just below the culvert under the road. This is where the water is the most comfortable at 105°. Many of the other pools are way too hot. A large mix of suits and no suits.

There are no services available on the premises. A campground is almost directly across FS 227. It is fourteen miles to all other services in Featherville.

Directions: From the town of Featherville, go east on FS 227 to the intersection with FS 094, then 2.2 miles farther on FS 227 and turn left after the culvert bridge to the parking area by the gate.

Source map: *Sawtooth National Forest.*

GPS: N 43 33.840 W 114 47.760

461   WILLOW CREEK HOT SPRINGS

● **East of the town of Featherville**

A series of primitive soaking pools in a lovely, small Alpine valley in the Sawtooth National Forest. Elevation 5,200 feet. Open all year.

Natural mineral water flows out of the ground at 125° and runs 100 yards across a gravel bar to join the creek. Volunteers have built an upper and lower series of rock-and-sand soaking pools where the water cools to 105° down to to 96° in the lower set of pools. The apparent local custom is clothing optional.

There is a pit toilet at the spring. There are no other services available at the spring, but there is a transfer station and corrals for equestrians at the trailhead. It is ten miles to other services in Featherville, and forty-seven miles to RV hookups.

Directions: From Featherville, drive seven miles east on FS 227 to Willow Creek, then two miles north on FS 008 to the campground and trailhead. The spring is 0.75 miles north on a moderate, well-maintained trail.

Source map: *Sawtooth National Forest.*

GPS: N 43 38.184 W 115 07.842

462   JOHNSON'S BRIDGE HOT SPRING

North of the town of Pine

Popular series of pools at the edge of the Boise River, both at the north and south ends of the bridge. Elevation 4,400 feet. Open all year.

Natural mineral water flows out of the springs on bank above the river. The 135° water flows through natural channels to the rock-and-sand pools at the river's edge. Several of the pools are at the north end of the bridge crossing, and there is a single pool just below the south bridge abutment. The water temperature can be controlled by mixing the hot water with cold river water, although the water swirls in and out of the pools making it impossible to maintain a single temperature. Bathing suits are required.

The springs are adjacent to Elks Flat Campground. It is four and one-half miles to gas in Pine and five miles to all other services in Featherville.

Directions: Drive 4.5 miles north of Pine to the campground and bridge.

GPS: N 43 32.388 W 115 17.340

Chris travels with his favorite model, his daughter Lexi who always brightens up a picture.

Middle Fork Boise River

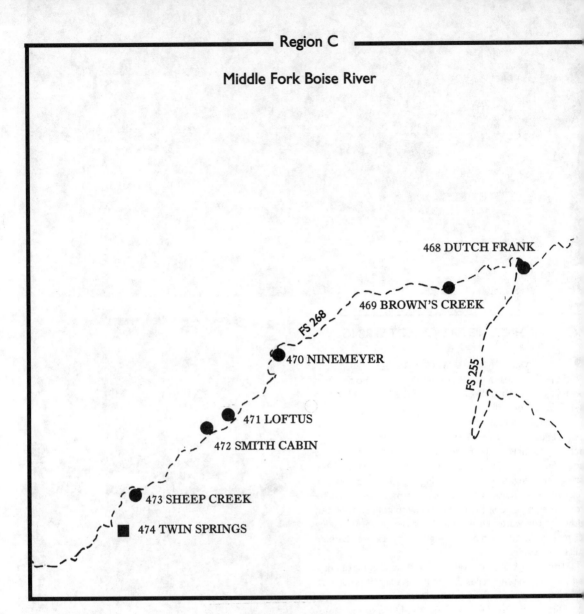

468 DUTCH FRANK

FS 268

469 BROWN'S CREEK

FS 255

470 NINEMEYER

471 LOFTUS

472 SMITH CABIN

473 SHEEP CREEK

474 TWIN SPRINGS

Middle Fork Boise River
Starting Point—town of Atlanta
Pages 136-142

Some of the springs in this area are open all year, weather permitting (these are noted). Many of the pools righ on the river are submerged during spring runoff and are not available until mid-July; those requiring fording the rive often are not available until mid-August. The season may last until early October.

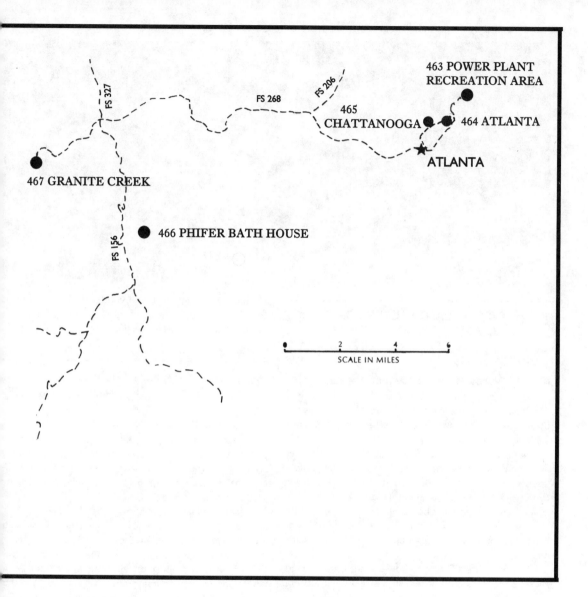

463 POWER PLANT
RECREATION AREA

FS 206

FS 327

FS 268

465
CHATTANOOGA

464 ATLANTA

ATLANTA

467 GRANITE CREEK

466 PHIFER BATH HOUSE

FS 156

2   4   6

SCALE IN MILES

Depending on which route you use to get to Atlanta, and on your type of vehicle, make sure you fill your gas tank in Boise, Idaho City, or Featherville. A store and some accommodations are available in Atlanta, but no gas. Source maps for most of the springs (some springs are not shown) are *Boise National Forest*; USGS *Atlanta East* and *Atlanta West*.

Phil Wilcox

463 POWER PLANT RECREATION AREA HOT SPRINGS

(see map on page 135)

● **Northeast of the town of Atlanta**

Several small pools adjacent to the Middle Fork of the Boise River and surrounded by wooded hillsides and open views of the Sawtooth Wilderness Area. Elevation 5,400 feet. Open all year.

Natural mineral water flows out of springs located near the river channel into several small, four- to six-foot pools, about a foot or so deep. As the pools are adjacent to the river, the water temperature can be regulated by adding river water but since the water temperature is about 100° this usually isn't necessary. The pools can be easily seen from the campground, so suits are recommended.

The pools are adjacent to Power Plant Campground, All other services are a little over a mile away in Atlanta.

Directions: Drive about 2.5 miles past Atlanta Hot Springs to the large flat "ball diamond" area at the entrance to the Power Plant Campground. The pools are located at the river's edge down a 25-foot embankment from the north end of the "ball diamond" area.

GPS: N 43 48.496   W 115 06.374

Besides the hot springs pool you might want to enjoy the "Frog Pond," a large warm swimming hole adjacent to *Atlanta Hot Springs*.

464 ATLANTA HOT SPRINGS

(see map on page 135)

● **Northeast of the town of Atlanta**

Rock-and-masonry soaking pool on a wooded plateau adjacent to a one-acre pond popular for summer swimming in the beautiful Sawtooth Mountains of Boise National Forest. Elevation 5,400 feet. Open all year; road access in winter could be difficult.

Natural mineral water flows out of a spring at 110° and cools as it travels to a nearby, volunteer-built pool, six feet by twelve feet, designed to be drained and quickly refilled after each use. The pool temperature is approximately 100°, depending on air temperature and wind conditions. The water drains into a large warm pond that locals call the "Frog Pond," which is used as a local swimming hole in the summer. This site is easily visible from the nearby road, so bathing suits are advisable.

No services are on the premises. It is one-half mile to the Power Plant Campground.

Directions: From Atlanta, follow FS 268 1.3 miles northwest. Pass a large pond on the right side of the road and park in a small turnout on the right side of the road immediately past the pond. The pool is visible from the parking area.

GPS: N 43 48.660   W 115 06.960

The Idaho Dippers

465   CHATTANOOGA HOT SPRINGS
(see map on page 135)

● **Northeast of the town of Atlanta**

Large, comfortable, sand-bottom pool at the foot of a geothermal cliff surrounded by the tree-covered slopes of Boise National Forest and a magnificent view of the Sawtooth Wilderness. Elevation 5,400 feet. Open all year.

Natural mineral water flows out of fissures in a 100-foot-high cliff at 120° and cools as it tumbles toward a volunteer-built, rock-and-sand soaking pool that retains a temperature of more than 100°. The apparent local custom is clothing optional.

There are no services on the premises. It is 0.75 miles to Power Point Campground.

Directions: From Atlanta follow FS 268 a little over a mile northeast toward Power Plant Campground. When a large pond and Atlanta Hot Springs are visible on the right, turn left toward the river and drive to the edge of the cliff. Park and walk the cliff trail northwest for about 60 yards until you can look down and see the pool. Several well-worn, steep paths lead down about 100 feet to the pool.

GPS: N 43 48.743 W 115 07.047

Jayson Loam

Phil Wilcox

The Idaho Dippers

466   PHIFER BATH HOUSE
(see map on page 135)

● **West of the town of Atlanta**

A scrap wood and plastic bathhouse set in the rugged mountains on the Middle Fork Boise River. Elevation 4,400 feet. Open all year; road access in winter could be difficult.

Natural mineral water flows out of a warm artesian well at 85° and is piped from the wellhead to the bath house that has a shower stall and tub. The apparent local custom is clothing optional.

It is eight miles to Queen's River Campground although many people camp along Phifer Creek.

Directions: Drive 17 miles west of Atlanta on FS 268 to the intersection of FS 327 and FS 156. Follow FS 156 south over the bridge, crossing the Middle Fork Boise River and immediately turn left on the first road. The short 0.25 mile road fords Phifer Creek and ends at the bathhouse. The ford is often washed out so just walk the quarter mile.

GPS: N 43 49.019 W 115 21.244

467   GRANITE CREEK HOT SPRING
(see map on page 135)

● **West of the town of Atlanta**

Large, deep pool located between FS 268 and the Middle Fork Boise River surrounded by wooded hills and considered by some to be one of the best. Elevation 4,200 feet. Open seasonally.

Natural mineral water flows out of several springs with temperatures up to 130° and runs through channels to a 12-foot by 20-foot, waist-deep, rock-and-sand pool located on the river's edge. Cold water from the river can be added to the pool to control the temperature. The pools are close to the road, so suits are advisable.

There are no services on the premises, and it is eleven miles to Idaho Outdoor Association Campground.

Directions: Drive 3.5 miles west on FS 268 from the intersection of FS 237 and FS 156. Continue about 3.5 miles and look for a large parking area cut into the hill on the right. The pool is easily visible from the road.

GPS: N 43 48.180 W 115 24.060

Photos by Phil Wilcox

468 DUTCH FRANK (ROARING RIVER) HOT SPRINGS
(see map on page 134)

● **Southwest of the town of Atlanta**

Several small pools at the bottom of a canyon on the edge of the Middle Fork Boise River. Elevation 4,100 feet. Open seasonally.

Natural mineral water flows from many small springs along several hundred yards of shoreline at temperatures up to 150°. Natural channels disperse the water into several small rock-and-sand pools that can be mixed with river water to adjust the hot water temperatures which range from 103-120°. As the river level lowers it might be necessary to dig out some new pools. Pools are highly visible from the road, and swimsuits are advisable.

There are no services on the premises and it is ten miles to Ninemeyer Campground.

Directions: Drive west from Atlanta on FS 268 for 22 miles to the junction of FS 255 at Roaring River. Turn south and cross the Middle Fork Boise River on FS 255 to a small parking area. Walk a hundred yards east to the highly visible thermal area.

GPS: N 43 47.340 W 115 26.040

469 BROWN'S CREEK HOT SPRING
(see map on page 134)

● **Southwest of the town of Atlanta**

Gorgeous photo-opportunity hot water shower on the opposite bank of the Middle Fork Boise River in a narrow canyon with steep hills and very fast water. This one is tricky to get to even at low water in late summer. Elevation 3,900 feet. Open seasonally.

Natural mineral water cascades from springs on a cliff above the pool at 120°, cooling as it flows down the cliff into a small six- by six-foot soaking pool at the base of the shower. The pool is easily visible from the road, and bathing suits are advised.

It is seven miles to the Ninemeyer Campground.

Directions: From Atlanta, drive 25 miles west on FS 268 look for hot water flowing down the cliff on the south side of the river. Parking is available in a turnoff directly opposite the spring. The river is swift at this point and caution should be used when fording the river.

GPS: N 43 46.740 W 115 29.160

Photo by Bob Seal

Bob Seal

Next to the hot pool volunteers have built a large, deep swimming hole.

470   NINEMEYER HOT SPRINGS
(see map on page 134)

● **Southwest of the town of Atlanta**

Small pool on the south side of the Middle Fork Boise River across from a campground with a wonderful adjacent swimming hole. Elevation 3,700 feet. Open seasonally (late August to October).

Several springs at 169° flow gently down the hillside to a riverside rock-and-sand pool that is presently about six by eight feet. The pool can be cooled by adding river water. It is easily visible from the road, and bathing suits are advised.

The springs are at Ninemeyer Campground.

Directions: From Atlanta drive west on FS 268 about 30 miles to Ninemeyer Campground. Look for the steamy hillside and pools directly across the river from the campground.

Source Map: USGS *Barber Flats.*
GPS: N 43 45.300 W 115 34.260

471   LOFTUS HOT SPRINGS
(see map on page 134)

● **Southwest of the town of Atlanta**

One of the more romantic spots with a warm shower, peaceful pools, and a grotto-like overhang lending a sense of privacy. Located above the road with a lovely view of the river and surrounding woods. Elevation 3,600 feet. Open all year.

Natural mineral water at 130° showers over the edge of an overhang into an eight-foot, very clean, sandy-bottom pool. The water in the upper pool, now at 105°, continues to flow into a lower six-foot pool supplied by the main pool runoff. The apparent local custom is clothing optional or by common consent.

Be aware: there is a great deal of poison oak, so watch where you put your towel.

It is four miles to Ninemeyer Campground.

Directions: From Atlanta, drive 34 miles west on FS 268. Look for a turnoff to the north and hot water flowing down the hill. The pools are a few yards up the hill from the parking area.

GPS: N 43 44.280 W 115 36.240

The Idaho Dippers

Photos by Phil Wilcox

472   SMITH CABIN HOT SPRINGS
(see map on page 134)

● **Southwest of the town of Atlanta**

Small rock pools on both sides of the Middle Fork Boise River. Elevation 3,500 feet. Open seasonally.

Natural mineral water flows out of the hillside above the river on the north bank and into volunteer-built, rock-and-sand pools on a gravel bar at the river's edge. On the south side, water flows to a small, shallow pool at the river's edge. These pools can only be accessed when the river is low (mid-August) and the pools are visible upstream from the ones on the north side. The hot water temperature of 138° can be controlled by adding river water. Bathing suits are advisable.

It is one-half mile to Troutdale Campground.

Directions: From Atlanta, drive west on FS 268 for about 35 miles. Look for a small rock pool on the near side of the river 0.7 miles after crossing a bridge over the river. Parking turnout is not available, but the road is wide here and traffic light.

Map Source: USGS *Sheep Creek* (pools on north side only).

GPS: N 43 43.200 W 115 37.020

473   SHEEP CREEK BRIDGE HOT SPRINGS
(see map on page 134)

● **Southwest of the town of Atlanta**

Shallow rock pool dug into a hillside several feet above the Middle Fork Boise River. Elevation 3,400 feet. Open all year.

Natural mineral water flows in a weak trickle down the hillside to a shallow rock pool laden with algae. The 142° water cools as it flows down the hillside, and air contributes to the rest of the cooling. Bathing suits advised.

It is two and one-half miles to Troutdale Campground.

Directions: From Atlanta, travel 38 miles to a bridge where the road recrosses the river. Park in a small turnout at the east end of the bridge. The spring is located several feet above the river, 50 yards downstream from the bridge.

GPS: N 43 41.760 W 115 39.480

474   TWIN SPRINGS

(see map on page 134)
HCR 35   **208 861-1226**
(Leave a message; calls will be returned
once or twice a week)
Boise, Idaho 83716
www.twinspringsidaho.com

Primitive but stylish rent-a-cabin resort in the central Idaho mountains located on the Middle Fork of the Boise River about halfway between Boise and Atlanta. The main store/bar at this historic resort once served as a store, school, lodging, kitchen, and home for several generations. Open all year.

The 150° natural mineral water is piped from the source spring to hot tubs, rental cabins, and steam sauna facilities. The hot tubs and sauna steam house are only available with cabin rental.

There are three cabins to choose from, each with two bedrooms, a full kitchen, and a deck with a private hot tub overlooking the Middle Fork of the Boise River. For larger groups there is an entire house with three full size bedrooms, a private hot tub, and a wood burning stove.

On-going improvements include a newly constructed water wheel, greenhouses, and a new trail system in the hills above the cabins for hiking, biking, and snowshoeing. There are several natural hot springs just miles up the road on the way to Atlanta. In addition, there is also fishing, gold panning, kayaking, tubing, snowmobiling, cross-country skiing, ATV riding, billiards, and hunting all close by.

Directions: From Boise take ID 21 towards Idaho City. Go past Lucky Peak Dam Approximately 6 miles later you will cross a large bridge. Immediately after crossing the bridge, turn right on FR 268 towards Atlanta. Drive 26.5 miles to the resort. Or from Atlanta, take FR 268 about 42 miles until you get to the resort.

475   GIVENS HOT SPRINGS

HC79 Box 103   **208 495-2000**
Melba, ID 83641

Rural plunge, picnic grounds, and RV park on agricultural plateau above the Snake River. Elevation 3,000 feet. Open all year.

Natural mineral water flows out of an artesian spring at 120° and is piped to a minimally chlorine-treated, indoor swimming pool and six indoor, private-space soaking pools that operate on a drain-and-fill basis. The swimming pool is maintained at a temperature of 92-93° in the winter and 99-100° in the summer. The temperature in the tubs is individually controllable, with temperatures ranging from 105-110°. Bathing suits are required.

Dressing rooms, suit and towel rentals, two cabins, snack bar, picnic grounds, softball diamond, volleyball, horseshoes, fishing on the Snake River, RV hookups, and overnight camping are available on the premises. Facilities available for family reunions. It is three miles to a boat dock, and eleven miles to all other services in Marsing. No credit cards are accepted.

Location: Eleven miles southeast of the town of Marsing on ID 78.

Courtesy of Givens Hot Springs

476 SAWTOOTH LODGE

130 N. Haines   208 259-3331
Grandjean, ID 83712
www.sawtoothlodge.com

Historic mountain resort situated at the end of the road on the edge of the magnificent Sawtooth Wilderness Area, a short walk from the South Fork Payette River. Elevation 5,100. Pool opens second week in June through Labor Day; resort is open Memorial Day through October.

Natural mineral water flows out of several springs with temperatures up to 150° and into an outdoor, chlorinated swimming pool maintained at approximately 80°. The pool is available to the public as well as to registered guests. Natural hot springs can also be found in the nearby river. Handicap facilities. Bathing suits are required.

Dressing rooms, restaurant serving mountain-style home cooking, rustic log cabins (with and without water, and with minimal electricity), overnight camping and a large group camping area for 100, and RV hookups are available on the premises. Horses, trail rides, pack trips, hunting, fishing, hiking all located nearby. It is forty-two miles to a store and service station in Stanley. Credit cards accepted. Call for reservations well in advance.

Directions: From the town of Lowman, go 22 miles east on ID 21, then follow signs 6 miles on gravel road to the lodge, 1 mile past Sacajawea Hot Springs.

477 SACAJAWEA HOT SPRINGS

●   West of the town of Grandjean

Popular, large geothermal area on the north bank of the South Fork of the Payette River in Boise National Forest. Elevation 5,000 feet. Open all year.

Natural mineral water flows out of many springs at temperatures up to 108° and cools as it cascades into a series of volunteer-built rock pools along the river's edge. Because the pools are visible from the road suits are advisable, although in the evenings there is more of a mix.

There are no services available on the premises although there is a camping area right nearby. It is one mile to a cafe, cabins, additional camping, and RV hookups at Sawtooth Lodge, and forty miles to a store and service station in Stanley.

Directions: From Lowman, drive 21 miles east on ID 21 to Grandjean turnoff (FS 524) on the right. Follow the gravel road 4.6 miles to Wapiti Creek Bridge. Look for springs on the right side of road, 0.6 miles past the bridge.

GPS: N 44 09.606 W 115 10.656

Chris Andrews

Phil Wilcox

478   BONNEVILLE HOT SPRINGS

● **West of the town of Grandjean**

Popular, semi-remote area on a tree-lined creek in Boise National Forest. Elevation 4,800 feet. Open all year.

Natural mineral water flows out of a multitude of springs with various temperatures up to 180°. Be careful not to step into any of the scalding runoff channels. There is one small, wooden bathhouse with an individual tub supplied with water from a nearby spring at a temperature of 103° and a cold water pipe to help cool the water. Soakers drain the tub after each use. There are also many volunteer-built, rock-and-sand soaking pools along the edge of the creek where the geothermal water can be mixed with cold water. Bathing suits are optional based on the desire of those present.

An adjacent campground with toilets is available for a fee. It is eight miles to a cafe, cabins, and RV hookups and forty miles to a store and service station in Stanley.

Directions: From Lowman, on SR 21, drive 19 miles northeast to Bonneville Campground (formerly Warm Springs Campground). From the north edge of the campground, follow the unmarked but well-worn path 0.25 miles to the geothermal area.

GPS: N 44 09.408   W 115 18.846

479   KIRKHAM HOT SPRINGS

● **East of the town of Lowman**

Popular geothermal area with many hot waterfalls and pools adjoining a National Forest campground on the South Fork of the Payette River. Elevation 4,200 feet. Open all year.

Natural mineral water flows out of many springs and fissures along the south bank of the river at temperatures up to 120° and cools as it cascades toward the river. Volunteers have built several rock-and-sand soaking pools in which temperatures can vary above or below 100° depending on air temperature and wind conditions. Bathing suits required.

Overnight camping is available in the adjoining campground. It is thirty-eight miles to a cafe, store, service station, and cabins and thirty-four miles to RV hookups, all located near Stanley.

Directions: From the town of Lowman, go 4.3 miles east on ID 21 and watch for the Kirkham Hot Springs Campground sign. Turn right into the campground

Source map: *Boise National Forest.*

GPS: N 44 04.320   W 115 32.580

There is now a charge to park while using the pools. However, if you camp at Bonneville, Kirkham, or Pine Flats, the host will give you a pass that allows you to park free at any of the three locations.

480 HAVEN HOT SPRINGS

7655 Highway 21   208 259-3344
Lowman, ID 83637
www.havenhotsprings.com

Motel rooms with outdoor private pools and swimming pool, and "food to die for," located in the Boise National Forest. Open all year; swimming pool closed after Labor Day.

Hot (148°) mineral water flows out of the springs into a large swimming pool which is approximately 99° all summer long. The pool is drained, cleaned and refilled once a week and is flow-through the rest of the time. The hot water is also used to fill the four private pools available with the rental of a motel room. The water temperature ranges between 105-110° and is controlled only by decreasing the flow of the water and the ambient air temperature. The water is changed after each soak. Bathing suits required in the swimming pool.

Four motel rooms with outdoor private pools, a three bedroom cabin, nine full-size RV spots with hookups, and a campground provide a wide variety of accommodations. A full service restaurant is right on the premises and is also available for private parties. All other services are found in Lowman, less than one mile away. Credit cards accepted.

481 PINE FLATS HOT SPRING

● **West of the town of Lowman**

Spectacular, geothermal cascade and cliffside soaking pool overlooking the South Fork of the Payette River in Boise National Forest. Elevation 4,100 feet. Open all year.

Natural mineral water with temperatures up to 125° flows from several springs on top of a 100-foot-high cliff, cooling as it spills and tumbles over the rocks. There is one volunteer-built, tarp-lined rock pool thirty feet above the river, immediately below a hot shower-bath that averages 104°. Other rock pools at the foot of the cliff have lower temperatures. The apparent local custom is clothing optional.

The hot springs are located one-third of a mile from the Pine Flats Campground and parking area. It is thirty-eight miles to a cafe, store, service station, and motel and twenty-seven miles to RV hookups, all near the town of Stanley.

Directions: From the west edge of Pine Flats campground, on SR 21 driving from Crouch toward Lowman, follow an unmarked but well-worn path 0.33 miles west down to and along a large riverbed and rock-and-sand bar. Look for geothermal water cascading down the cliff onto the bar.

Source map: *Boise National Forest.*
GPS: N 44 03.720 W 115 41.100

Jayson Loam

A short walk from the Pine Flats Campground puts your feet in a warm-water runoff and the lower pools. An easy climb takes you up to the wonderful water fall and deeper hot pool near the top of the cliffs.

482A LITTLE ANDERSON HOT SPRING

● **East of the town of Crouch**

A volunteer-dug pool hidden in the trees on the banks of Anderson Creek on the edge of Boise National Forest. Elevation 3,200 feet. Open all year.

Natural mineral water comes up through the sandy bottom near the back of a concrete block pool at about 101°. Swimsuits optional.

Hot Springs campground is quite close and all other services can be found either in Garden Valley or in Crouch. The spring is on private property so take extra care of the spring and be sure to pack out what you bring in.

Directions: Take the Banks-Lowman Highway from Crouch east to Garden Valley. Turn left just west of town on FR 668 (Granite Basin Rd.) about 0.2 miles west of the Chevron station in Garden Valley. Continue 2 miles to FS 669, Anderson Creek Rd. (gravel) heading north to Anderson Creek, and take the right fork. After crossing the bridge over the creek, look for a trail along the creek to the right. The hot springs is 200 yards or so downstream.

Source map: *Boise National Forest* (spring not on map).
GPS: N 44 06.322 W 115 55.734

Marjorie Young

Photo of New Zealand hot springs enthusiast, Sally Jackson, taken by "Hot Springs" Harley who deserves credit for building and maintaining many of our hot springs.

482B HOT SPRINGS CAMPGROUND

● **East of the town of Crouch**

The cement foundation of a long-gone bathhouse and a large, volunteer-built soaking pool intended to use some of the continuing hot-water flow. Located on a riverbank across the highway from a National Forest campground.

Natural mineral water flows out of several springs at 105° and into a volunteer-built, shallow, rock-and-sand pool near the south side of the highway. Additional pools are often built along the river's edge but disappear during high water. Bathing suits are advisable.

Overnight camping is available on the premises directly across the road. All other services are four miles away in Crouch.

Directions: From the town of Crouch, go 4 miles east toward Lowman. Look for Hot Springs Campground on your left 1 mile after entering Forest Service land (posted). Park in the large turnoff on your right and follow the gravel path and steps down to the pool.

Source map: Boise National Forest.
GPS: N 44 03.240 W 115 54.420

All the concrete, piping and other supplies had to be carried by volunteers up a very steep path. They not only built the pools but come back every weekend to drain and clean them. Thanks.

483   SKINNY DIPPER HOT SPRINGS

East of the town of Banks

Large, wonderful, volunteer-built rock-and-mortar soaking pools on a very steep hillside overlooking the south fork of the Payette River. Elevation 3,300 feet. Open all year.

Natural mineral water flows out of the source spring at 160° where it piped, along with water from a cold source, through an elaborate series of pipes to three pools that side-step down the steep hillside. All were built and are maintained by local volunteers. Valves control the temperature in each pool and drain off the excess hot water. The lowest pool is approximately sixteen feet in diameter and has an underwater bench to sit on. Swimsuits are rare.

There are no services available on the premises, but all services are available four miles away in Banks. Places to camp can be found within fifteen miles in any direction.

Directions: From Banks, on Hwy 55, go to mile post 4 on the Crouch-Lowman Highway. There is a good pull-out area next to the river. Across the highway look for a trail that heads up the mountain. You know you are on the right trail if you have to step over a yellow power line support cable. Continue up the switch backs until the main trail angles east through a gully, then across a ridge. From here the trail angles down to the spring. The trail is around 0.5 of a mile but is extremely steep and very slippery when wet, and dry and dusty in the summer.

Source map: *Boise National Forest* (spring not on map).

GPS: N 44 05.460 W 116 02.994

Photo above and below by "Hot Springs Harley"
Photo on left by Chris Andrews

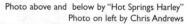

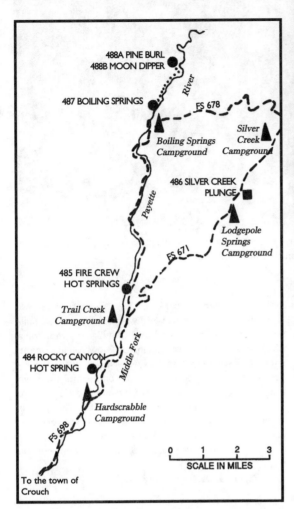

488A PINE BURL
488B MOON DIPPER

River

487 BOILING SPRINGS

FS 678

Silver
Creek
Campground

Boiling Springs
Campground

Payette

486 SILVER CREEK
PLUNGE

Lodgepole
Springs
Campground

FS 671

485 FIRE CREW
HOT SPRINGS

Trail Creek
Campground

Middle Fork

484 ROCKY CANYON
HOT SPRING

Hardscrabble
Campground

FS 698

To the town of
Crouch

0   1   2   3
SCALE IN MILES

Sally Jackson

484   ROCKY CANYON HOT SPRING
(see map)

● **North of the town of Crouch**

Primitive hot spring across the river on the Middle Fork of the Payette in Boise National Forest. Elevation 3,600 feet. Open all year; fording the river should only be done in late summer or early fall.

Natural mineral water flows out of a spring at 120°, then down a steep slope toward the river. To reach the spring, you must ford the river, which might not be safe during high water. Volunteers have built two soaking pools about midway up the mountain and a piece of pipe protruding from the dam of the upper pool creates a shower at about 103°. Pools are visible from the road, so it's your choice as to whether you wear a suit or not.

There are no services available on the premises. It is one and one-half miles to Hardscrabble Campground, and ten miles to all other services in Crouch.

Directions: From Crouch, take FS 698 about 12.5 miles. Drive 1.6 miles past the bridge and park in a turnout on your left. The turnout is about 1.5 miles north of the Hardscrabble Campground. Pools are across the river, and fording the river should only be done in late summer or early fall.

Source map: *Boise National Forest.*
GPS: N 44 15.144 W 115 53.448

Nick Hertelendy

485   FIRE CREW HOT SPRINGS
(see map on page 148)

● **North of the town of Crouch**

Several pools in a winding river canyon at the edge of the Middle Fork of the Payette River in Boise National Forest. Elevation 3,800 feet. Open all year.

Natural mineral water flows from springs at temperatures above 120° into a fifteen-foot, rock-edged pool adjacent to the river. By moving the rocks, cold river water can be added to the pool to adjust the temperature. If the river water is too low to let in cold water be very careful getting into the soaking pool as the water may be extremely hot. The apparent local custom is clothing optional.

It is one-half mile to Trail Creek Campground and fifteen miles to Crouch for all other services.

Directions: From Crouch, drive north on FS 698 toward Boiling Springs. About 0.3 miles past the junction with FS 671 look for a dirt road, #698L8, on the river side of FS 698. Follow the road for a short distance to a turn-around and parking area. The pools are located on the upstream end of the parking area. The road is not recommended for RVs or trailers; high clearance vehicles recommended. If you decide to walk in, it is only about 0.25 of a mile.

GPS: N 44 16.914 W 115 52.440

Chris Andrews

Courtesy of Silver Creek Plunge

Phil Wilcox

486   SILVER CREEK PLUNGE
2345 Silver Creek Rd   208 870-0586
(see map on page 148)
■ **Garden Valley, ID 83622**

Remote, mountain resort surrounded by Boise National Forest. Elevation 4,700 feet. Operated partially on National Forest Systems Lands. Open all year; snowmobile access in winter.

Natural mineral water flows out of a spring at 101° directly into an outdoor swimming pool that is maintained at 95°. The pool operates on a flow-through basis, requiring a minimum of chlorination. It is available to the public as well as to registered guests. Bathing suits are required.

Dressing rooms, convenience store, snack bar, cabins (with advance reservations), and overnight camping are available on the premises. It is twenty-two miles to a service station, and RV hookups. Electricity is generated on a limited basis. During snowy weather the owners provide a snow-cat shuttle service from about one mile after the pavement stops to the resort. Credit cards are accepted.

Directions: From the town of Crouch, go north 14 miles on FS 698 (Middle Fork Road), then bear northeast on FS 671 for 9 miles to the plunge. Follow the signs.

Source map: *Boise National Forest.*

487   BOILING SPRINGS
(see map on page 148)

●   **North of the town of Crouch**

Large, geothermal water flow on the Middle Fork of the Payette River in Boise National Forest. Elevation 4,200 feet. Open all year.

Natural mineral water flows out of a cliff at more than 130° into a pond adjacent to the Boiling Springs guard station. The water cools as it flows through a ditch to join the river. Summer volunteers usually build a rock-and-mud dam at the point where the water is cool enough for soaking or where river water can be added. The best pool to soak in is the one under the overhang, at 108°, as the riverside pools are usually quite shallow. Because of the nearby campground, bathing suits are advisable.

No services are available on the premises. It is one-quarter of a mile to Boiling Springs Campground and nineteen miles to all other services in Crouch.

Directions: From the north edge of Boiling Springs Campground, follow the path 0.25 miles to the rental cabin (which used to be the guard station) and the spring. You might also like to visit Moon Dipper and Pine Burl Hot Springs which are on the same trail.

Source map: *Boise National Forest.*
GPS: N 44 21.810 W 115 44.988

Nick Hertelendy

488A   MOON DIPPER HOT SPRING AND
488B   PINE BURL HOT SPRING
(see map on page 148)

● **North of the town of Crouch**

Two lovely, remote and primitive hot springs on the bank of Dash Creek, very close together in Boise National Forest. Elevation 4,200 feet. Open all year.

Natural mineral water flows out of the cliff face at 130° and directly into volunteer-built, rock soaking pools. Water temperature in the pools is controlled by mixing cold creek water with the hot water. Moon Dipper, a large, sandy-bottom pool, has a nice canyon view, while Pine Burl offers a small, romantic spot for two. The apparent local custom is clothing optional.

No services are available on the premises. It is a two-mile hike to overnight camping and twenty-one miles to all other services.

Note: There are several more primitive hot springs with the potential for volunteer-built soaking pools further upstream from Moon Dipper and Pine Burl. However, all of them require that the river be forded many times with a high risk of losing the faint, unmarked path. Consult a Boise National Forest ranger before attempting to hike to any of these springs.

Directions: About 0.25 mile from the former Boiling Springs guard station (now a rental cabin) follow the well-used (sometimes slippery), easy, flat, unmarked lower trail for a two-mile hike to the springs. You may get your feet wet. Just after passing a hot water source on your left (too hot), and a nice sandy beach on your right you will come to Dash Creek. Go left up the creek for a few yards and Moon Dipper will appear. Pine Burl is a few more yards up Dash Creek.

Source maps: *Boise National Forest*, USGS *Boiling Springs, Idaho* (springs not on quad).

GPS: N 44 22.909 W 115 50.652 (Moon Dipper)
    N 44 22.956 W 115 50.487 (Pine Burl)

Photos by Nick Hertelendy

● **Northeast of the town of Lowman**

Small hot spring situated along the river bank in the River of No Return Wilderness and requiring less than a mile hike to get to. Elevation 5,800 feet. Open all year.

Natural mineral water at 103° comes up through the sandy bottom of a small, shallow rock-lined pool. Stretching out is the only way to get most of your body covered. Clothing optional.

Two campgrounds are less than a mile away, one back where you parked off the right fork, and the other larger campground off the end of the left fork. All other services can be found in Lowman or Stanley.

Directions: On ID 21, drive 37 miles northeast of Lowman (21 miles northwest of Stanley) and turn west on FR 82/579 signed to Bruce Meadows and Boundary Creek. At 8 miles a sign marks the turnoff to Fir Creek Campground. Turn north on FR 568 and drive 15 miles to a junction where the right fork (at the end of a landing strip) will take you to Dagger Falls and a small campground where you can park. Follow the path along the Middle Fork Salmon River upstream past the falls about 0.5 mile to the mouth of Dagger Creek. Continue following the creek a short way upstream to the pool.

Source map: *Salmon-Challis National Forest* (spring not on map).

Note: Those of you who are hearty hikers and adventurers might want to try Trail Flat and Sheepeater Hot Springs. The best directions can be found in Evie Litton's book, *Hiking: Hot Springs in the Pacific Northwest*, 3rd edition.

GPS: N 44 30.960 W 115 17.700

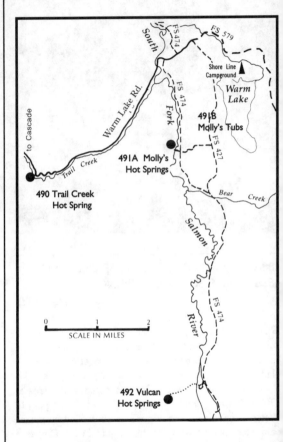

(see map on page 152)

● **West of Warm Lake**

Small, beautiful hot spring pools in a narrow canyon down a steep sixty-yard path from a paved highway in Boise National Forest. Elevation 5,654 feet. Open all year.

Natural mineral water flows out of a fissure in the rocks adjoining Trail Creek at 125°. Volunteers have built two rock-and-sand soaking pools on the edge of the creek where the temperature can be controlled by changing the amount of cold creek water admitted through a four-inch pipe. The upper pool is eight feet by twelve feet and about two feet deep. The water temperature in the lower pool, which is about six feet around, is controlled by diverting water from the creek directly into the pool. The apparent local custom is clothing optional.

No services are available on the premises. It is two miles to a campground, seven miles to gas, cafe, cabins, and phone at Warm Lake Lodge (open Memorial Day to October 15), and twenty-two miles to all other services in Cascade.

Directions: From Highway 55 at Cascade, take the Warm Lake Highway 19.2 miles northeast and look for an especially large parking area on the south side of the road about 0.4 mile east of Milepost 61. From the west edge of this parking area, the pool is visible at the bottom of Trail Creek canyon. There is no maintained trail, so be careful scrambling down the 60-yard steep path.

Source map: *Boise National Forest.*
GPS: N 44 37.638 W 115 45.024

Photos by The Idaho Dippers

Chris Andrews

Skip Hill

491A   MOLLY'S TUBS

(see map on page 152)

● **West of Warm Lake**

A much-used collection of bathtubs on the South Fork of the Salmon River in Boise National Forest. Elevation 5,200 feet. Open all year.

Natural mineral water flows out of several springs at approximately 136° and is piped through hoses to eight bathtubs. Buckets are used for adding cold water from the nearby river. The tubs are lined up in two groups so you can have relative privacy if desired. Buckets and rubber stoppers for the tubs were there at last report. There are also pools at the river's edge that are rebuilt each year after the high water level recedes. The apparent local custom is clothing optional.

There are no services available on the premises. It is one and one-half miles to Shoreline campground, three and one-half miles to Warm Lake Lodge (open Memorial Day to October 15), and twenty-four miles to all other services in Cascade.

Directions: From the intersection of FS 22 (paved) and FS 474 (gravel), go 1.3 miles south on FS 474 to a pull-out on right. (From Warm Lake, the second Stolle Meadows sign is 474S.) Follow a steep path down to the tubs.

Source map: *Boise National Forest.*
GPS: N 44 38.496 W 115 41.664

491B   MOLLY'S HOT SPRING

(see map on page 152)

● **West of Warm Lake**

A sandy-bottom pool on the side of a steep, geothermal hillside overlooking the South Fork of the Salmon River in Boise National Forest. Locals named this one "the Duke" in honor of repeated visits from John Wayne and Robert Mitchum. Elevation 5,400 feet. Open all year.

Natural mineral water flows out of several springs at temperatures up to 120° and is transported downhill by a variety of pipes and hoses. Water temperature in the volunteer-built pool is controlled by diverting or combining the hotter and cooler flows. Additional volunteer work could produce an excellent chest-deep pool. The apparent local custom is clothing optional.

No services are available on the premises. It is two miles to overnight camping at shoreline, four miles to gas, cafe, store, cabins, and phone at Warm Lake Lodge (open Memorial Day to October 15), and twenty-five miles to all other services in Cascade.

Directions: From the intersection of FS 22 (paved) and FS 474 (a signed gravel road to Stole Meadows), go 1.9 miles south on FS 474 to the intersection with a road where a sign directs you east to Warm Lake. The road leading west from this intersection has been blocked to vehicle traffic, but it is passable on foot. Park and walk west on this blocked road 300 yards, cross the old bridge and immediately turn right onto a trail that is just above the fallen trees at the waters edge. Follow the trail 100 yards north to the thermal area. This spring is 0.4 of a mile further than Molly's Tubs.

Source map: *Boise National Forest.*
GPS: N 44 38.004 W 115 41.784

Bob Seal

492   VULCAN HOT SPRINGS
(see map on page 152)

● **South of Warm Lake**

Still popular, geothermal creek pools in the Boise National Forest which seem to be getting hotter each year. The pools are considered by many to be too hot to even bother with. The trees, once insect-ravaged, seem to be making a comeback. Elevation 5,600 feet. Open all year.

Natural mineral water flows out of many small, bubbling springs at boiling temperatures (138° in places), creating a substantial hot creek that gradually cools as it runs through the woods toward the South Fork of the Salmon River. Volunteers had built a log dam across this creek at a point where the water had cooled somewhat. This dam has been partly wiped out by high-water runoff, but some pools remain. The one-mile trail to the springs is no longer maintained. One mile south of Stole Meadows there is an unmarked, unofficial camping area where the trail head to the springs begins. It is seven miles to a Forest Service campground and thirty-two miles to all other services.

Directions: At the west edge of the camping area is a log footbridge built by the Corps of Engineers. Cross this bridge and follow the path across two more log bridges. It is approximately one mile to the dam and pool.

Source maps: *Boise National Forest*; USGS *Warm Lake, Idaho.*

GPS: N 44 34.080 W 115 41.700

Skip Hill

493   SUGAH (MILE 16) HOT SPRING

● **North of Warm Lake**

A sweetie of a remote soaking pool for two, located on the edge of the South Fork of the Salmon River in Payette National Forest. Elevation 4,800 feet. Open all year.

Natural mineral water flows out of a spring at 115° and cools as it goes through a makeshift pipe to the beautifully constructed rock-and-masonry pool at the river's edge. Pool temperature is controlled by diverting the hot water and/or by adding a bucket of cold river water. The apparent local custom is clothing optional.

There are no services available on the premises. There is a campground within two miles, and it is forty miles to all other services.

Directions: From the intersection of FS 22 (paved) and FS 474, signed to Kassel and Yellow Pine, go north on FS 474 along the South Fork of the Salmon River for 16 miles to the spring. At 1.6 miles past Poverty Flats Campground, there is a small (two-car) turnout on the side of the road toward the river. Look for an unmarked, set of wooden stairs and path down to the pool which has been carefully formed into switchbacks by volunteers to prevent erosion.

Source maps: *Payette National Forest; Boise National Forest.*

GPS: N 44 50.814 W 115 41.826

494 COUNCIL MOUNTAIN (LAUREL) HOT SPRINGS

(see map)

● **Southeast of the town of Council**

Several primitive, thermal springs fed by water cascading over the rocks in a wooded canyon at the end of a rugged, two-mile hike in the Payette National Forest. Elevation 4,300 feet. Open all year.

Natural mineral water flows out of several springs at temperatures up to 134° and into progressively cooler, volunteer-built soaking pools along the bottom of Warm Springs Creek. A log dam helps form the largest soaking pool. Pool temperatures rise as the river water recedes. Clothing optional.

There are no services on the premises. It is two miles to Cabin Creek Campground, although there is open ground to camp on the way to the springs, and twenty-three miles to all other services in Council.

Directions: Drive south of the town of Council on US 95 to milemarker 130, turning east onto a gravel road that follows the Middle Fork Weiser River for 9 miles until you see a small sign indicating trail number 203. Follow 203 two miles north straight uphill to the springs, being very careful where the trail crosses the creek as the water is often very hot.

Source map: *USGS Council Mountain.*

GPS: N 44 40.134 W 116 18.336

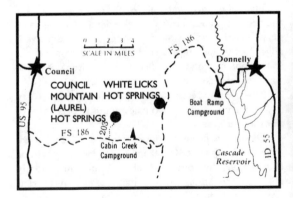

To the people around the the town of Council, this wonderful place to soak is known simply as "the springs."

Photos by Chris Andrews

495   WHITE LICKS HOT SPRINGS
(see map on page 156)

●   **West of the town of Donnelly**

A large, geothermal seep serving two small bathhouses in an unofficial camping area at a wooded site surrounded by Payette National Forest. Elevation 4,800 feet. Open all year.

Natural mineral water flows out of many small springs at temperatures up to 120°, supplying two small, wood shacks, each containing a cement tub. Each tub is served by two pipes, one bringing in 110° water, the other bringing in 80° water. The tub temperature is controlled by plugging up the pipe bringing in the water not desired. Soakers are expected to drain the tub after each use. Bathing suits are not required inside the bathhouses.

A picnic area and camping are available on the premises. It is sixteen miles to all other services.

Directions: From ID 55 in Donnelly, turn west on Rosebury Rd. Cross the Cascade Reservoir bridge. Turn left on Norwood Road and turn right onto Tamarack Falles Rd. After crossing the bridge right before Tamarack Store turn right onto West Mountain Rd. which almost immediately becomes gravel, bear left at the "Y", and follow FS 186 as it starts north, curves west, and then goes south. Watch for the hot spring on the west side of FS 186, 4.2 miles south of the intersection of FS 245 (Middle Fork Weisser Rd.) and FS 186. Bathhouses almost immediately visible on the right after crossing creek. It is 10.5 miles from the "Y."

GPS: N 44 40.932 W 116 13.752

Chris Andrews

Bob Seal

Wally Deitrich

496   OXBOW HOT SPRINGS

● **Northwest of the town of Cambridge**

A good pull on a row boat, or better yet, a motor boat will bring you across the 300-yard wide Oxbow Reservoir to a private pool located in Hells Canyon where ten months out of the year the weather lives up to its name. Located on the Idaho side of Oxbow Reservoir. Elevation, 1,900 feet. Open all year. Privately owned, publicly shared—do your best to keep it clean.

Natural mineral water is piped to a five by eight-foot pool made from the travertine rock which also forms the cliffs in the area. A nice deck is along side the pool and another pipe brings in the cold water to help create your favorite temperature. Clothing optional.

Directions: From the town of Cambridge take ID 71 towards Hells Canyon. Travel north along Brownlee Reservoir and Brownlee Dam until you reach a bridge crossing Oxbow Reservoir. Travel 8 miles past the bridge to a small boat ramp. This is the launch site. Head across the reservoir aiming for the canyon directly across from the boat ramp. There is a trail from the beach leading up to the hot spring.

Source map: *Payette National Forest* (west).
GPS: N 44 56.658 W 116 50.040

Chris Andrews

Author Evie Litton preparing to take the plunge.

Bob Seal

Courtesy of The Lodge at Riggins Hot Springs

497 ZIM'S HOT SPRINGS
PO Box 314   208 347-9447
New Meadows, ID 83654

Family owned plunge and picnic grounds in an agricultural valley surrounded by pines. The Little Salmon River runs through the property and the spectacular Granite Mountains provide the view. Elevation 4,200 feet. Open all year.

Natural mineral water flows out of an artesian well at 151° and is cooled as it is sprayed into the chlorine-treated pools. The temperature in the outdoor swimming pool ranges from 90-100° and from 103-106° in the outdoor soaking pool. Bathing suits are required.

Locker rooms, snacks, picnic area, overnight camping, and RV hookups are available on the premises. Fishing and winter sports are close by. A store, service station, and motel are located within four miles. Visa and MasterCard are accepted.

Directions: From the town of New Meadows, take US 95 four miles north, then follow signs to the plunge.

498 THE LODGE AT RIGGINS HOT SPRINGS
PO Box 1247   208 628-3785
Riggins, ID 83549

Secluded 155-acre luxury resort on the banks of the Salmon River, ten miles east of Riggins. Elevation 1,800 feet. Open all year. Open only to groups, except for occasional weekends (call for dates).

Natural mineral water flows out of an artesian well at 140° and is piped to the recently remodeled swimming pool and enclosed spa. Water temperature in the flow-though spa is maintained at 105-108° without chlorination. Water temperature in the flow-through pool is maintained at 92-97° with a minimum of chlorination. Bathing suits are required.

Luxurious rooms with private baths are available in the main lodge and in a new three unit cabin. Meals and beverages included with the room rate. A stocked trout pond, a bathhouse with game room, and a conference center are available on the premises. Access to the Salmon River whitewater provides rafting, steelhead fishing, and jetboat excursions. Horses can be rented nearby. Credit cards accepted.

Phone for rates, reservations, and directions.

499 FRENCH CREEK (CABLE CAR) HOT SPRINGS

● **East of the town of Riggins**

Bring your own raft, kayak or canoe to reach this log bathhouse situated on a hillside high above the Salmon Rive in the Nez Perce National Forest. Elevation 2,500 feet. Open all year, depending on weather conditions and high river runoff.

Steamy, hot natural mineral water is piped into a hollowed out ponderosa log with just enough room for two very close friends. The 100° water makes for a perfect soak on a hot summer day and the bathhouse roof helps keep off the hot sun with large windows letting in the light. Swimsuits unnecessary.

All services are approximately nineteen miles away in Riggins. Campgrounds are within seven miles, but I would treat myself to a stay at rustic Burgdorf Hot Springs, about twenty-six miles away, which can also supply you with a nice hot soak.

Directions: From the town of Riggins take the Salmon River Road east 18.5 miles (all but the last 6 miles is paved) watching for a concrete piling on the far side of the river that used to be a support for a cable car. Park in the pullout 0.1 mile after crossing French Creek where you can scramble down to the river and put in your boat. A life jacket is highly recommended. Head straight across to the tiny beach. There is also another beach upstream. Trails go off from either place to join the main trail near the old tram site. The trail heads straight up hill for less than a mile bringing you first to an old, often bat-filled mining tunnel, and then to the log bathhouse which sits right over the spring. As the trail goes from the beach up the hill it passes through an old cabin site and orchard. In season there are apples, apricots, and all the blackberries you can eat. You may have to argue with a bear for the blackberries, so be careful. Also, watch out for poison ivy and rattlesnakes.

Source maps: *Payette National Forest* and *Nez Perce National Forest* (springs not on map).

GPS: N 45 25.884 W 116 00.918

This was a trip taken by some very dedicated hot springers—Sally Jackson from New Zealand who writes books about hot springs there, seen below with Chris Andrews and above with Stephanie and Chuck Ensign, known affectionately as The Idaho Dippers.

Chris Andrews, without whom this new edition would not have been possible, takes time to enjoy what he calls "a great soak" in the mine which at this point has no bats. If they return soaking becomes a dirty, smelly business.

Upper photo by Chris Andrews
Lower photo by Stephanie Ensign

One of the best views from the Hot Springs is of the surrounding meadows where Burgdorf and the Fish and Game Department have joined together to create a protected calving ground for the elk. While you cannot go out in the meadow, bring a pair of binoculars and enjoy watching the wildlife. You will also enjoy some of the great woodworking that the past and current managers have created.

500　BURGDORF HOT SPRINGS

208 636-3036

McCall, ID 83638

Picturesque, mountain-rustic resort without electricity, surrounded by Payette National Forest. Elevation 6,000 feet. Open all year. During the winter you can get there by snowmobile or cross-country skis. The pools are open twenty-four hours a day to registered guests and 10 AM until dark for day use.

Natural mineral water flows out of a spring at 112° and directly into and through a fifty by seventy-five-foot sandy-bottom swimming pool that averages 104° at the feed end and 98° at the outflow. The pool is about five-feet deep and requires no chemical treatment. There is also a small children's pool. Bathing suits are required during the daytime (available for rent). Alcohol is never permitted around the pool and no dogs are allowed.

Fifteen cabins with outdoor plumbing are available on the premises. Called "camping in a cabin" you need to bring your own bedding, food, cooking utensils, etc. Pack it in and out, and bring only biodegradable toiletries.

There is also a small store with cold drinks, snacks, and some grocery items.

Overnight camping is within one-quarter of a mile. Check with the Payette National Forest Service in McCall for information. It is thirty miles to McCall and all other services. Hiking, skiing, snowmobiling, and boating are nearby. No credit cards accepted.

You must write or phone first for reservations and information on what to bring.

This couple brought their older daughter as an infant and now her sister joins these dedicated soakers.

MONTANA

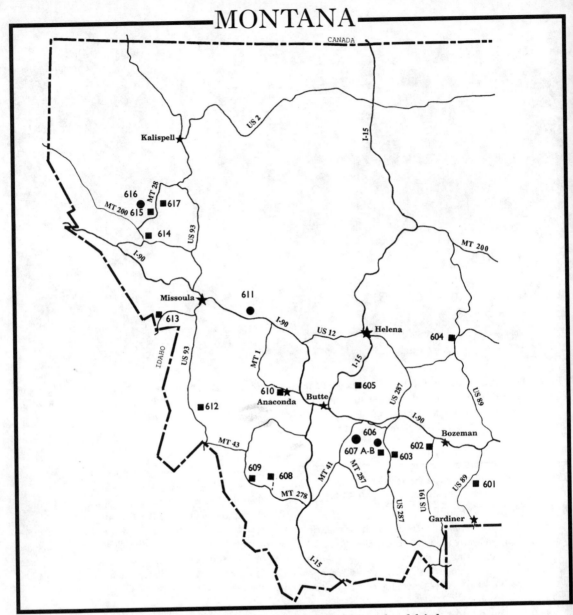

CANADA

Kalispell ★

616 ● ■617
MT 200 615 ■

■ 614

611 ●

Missoula ★
■ 613

604 ■

Helena ★

610 ■★
Anaconda

Butte ★

■ 605

■ 612

606 ●
607 A-B ■
■ 603

602 ■
Bozeman ★

609 ■ ■ 608

601 ■

Gardiner ★

MT 28
US 93
US 2
I-15
MT 200
US 12
MT 1
I-90
IDAHO
US 93
MT 43
I-90
I-15
US 287
US 89
MT 41
MT 287
MT 278
US 287
US 191
US 89
I-15

This map was designed to be used with a standard highway map.

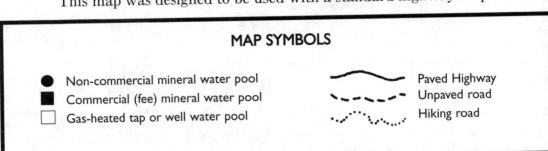

MAP SYMBOLS

● Non-commercial mineral water pool
■ Commercial (fee) mineral water pool
□ Gas-heated tap or well water pool

〜 Paved Highway
--- Unpaved road
⋯ Hiking road

**601 CHICO HOT SPRINGS RESORT
AND DAY SPA**
PO Drawer 29   406 333-4933
Pray, MT 59065
www.chicohotsprings.com

Large, year-round resort established in 1900, surrounded by Gallatin National Forest. Elevation 5,200 feet. Open all year.

Natural mineral water flows out of several springs at 118° and is piped into a nearly Olympic-size, open-air pool maintained at 96°. The adjacent covered soaking pool averages 105°. One private-space hot tub, rented separately, is held at 105°. All pools operate on a flow-through basis and are available to the public as well as to resort guests. There is a wheelchair ramp through the poolside grill, and rooms are handicap accessible. Bathing suits required.

Accommodations are available in the Main Lodge, the newer Lower Lodge, motel, log cabins, and condominiums. The resort offers dining in the Chico Inn and more casual fare in the Poolside Grille, a saloon with live entertainment on weekends. Also offered are horseback riding, mountain bike and cross-country ski rentals, dogsled treks, and summer raft trips. It is three miles to a store with gas pumps and about eight miles to a full-service campground. Major credit cards accepted.

Directions: Located approximately 23 miles south of Livingston and 31 miles north of Gardiner (the north entrance to Yellowstone Park). From the town of Emigrant on US 89, turn southeast on Murphy Lane (SR 362), go 0.8 miles to the stop sign, then left on East River Rd. (SR 540). Go 0.5 miles, then take the first right onto the Chico Road (SR 542). Resort is 1.6 miles up the road.

**602   BOZEMAN HOT SPRINGS
SPA AND FITNESS CENTER**
81123 Gallatin Rd.   **406 586-6492**
Bozeman, MT 59718
www.bozemansprings.com

Tree-shaded ever-expanding family vacation stop in the Gallatin Valley. Elevation 4,500 feet. Open all year.

Natural mineral water flows out of a spring at 141° and is piped to nine pools in the indoor pool building and to the outdoor pools. The swimming pool is maintained at 90°, and the adjoining soaking pools are maintained at varying temperatures ranging from 90-104°. There is also a 60° cold pool. The inside pools change out water five times a day and are drained and cleaned nightly, eliminating the need for chlorine. An outside pool is kept at a comfortable 100° in the winter and at cooler temperatures during the summer. Pools are available to the public as well as to registered guests. Bathing suits required.

On the premises is a dry and wet sauna (kept at 140°), a juice bar, day care, and a full fitness center. Personalized treatments are available at the in-house spa and include skin care, body treatments, massage therapy and anti-aging treatments. It is one mile to a restaurant and service station and eight miles to a motel. A KOA campground is adjacent to the property. Credit cards accepted.

Location: Nine miles from the Belgrade exit off of I 90. Approximately 5 miles southwest of Bozeman and less than an hour to Big Sky Ski Resort.

People have been coming to these springs since the 1870s. Enjoy their unusual dry sauna called the Sahara Desert which includes fiber optic lighting, or the Amazon Rain Forest room where you can relax with hot water sprinkling out of the ceiling imitating an actual rain for-

Photo courtesy of Norris Hot Springs

Skip Hill

603   NORRIS HOT SPRINGS

PO Box 2916   406 685-3303
Rt. 84
Norris, MT 59745

Small RV park in foothills below Tobacco Root Mountains. Elevation 5,000 feet. Open all year; days and times vary (Wednesday through Sunday, noon to 10 PM). Be sure to call to check on open times.

Natural mineral water flows out of artesian springs at 115° and provides a continual flow-through in the outdoor swimming pool. Water temperature varies between 102-108° in the winter and 112° in the summer, depending on the weather. An electrical aeration system pumps the water into the air to help cool it in the summer. The water contains no sulfur, and no chemical treatment is necessary because the pool operates on a flow-through basis. Easy entry for handicap accessibility. Bathing suits required. (No glass, no soap or shampoo.)

A store, changing rooms, and a picnic area are available on the premises. It is one-quarter mile to a cafe, mini-mart and service station in Norris and seventeen miles south to a motel. No credit cards accepted.

Directions: From US 287 in the town of Norris, go 0.25 miles east on MT 84.

604   SPA HOT SPRINGS MOTEL

PO Box 370
                             406 547-3366

White Sulphur Springs, MT 59645

Modern resort at the foot of the Castle Mountains. Elevation 5,100. Open all year.

Natural mineral water flows out of a spring at 120° and is piped to two pools that operate on a flow-through basis, requiring no chemical treatment. The pools are drained, cleaned, and refilled every night. The outdoor swimming pool is maintained at 94° in the summer and 102° in the winter. The indoor soaking pool is maintained at 105-106°. The deck around the pools, and the entire facility are geothermally heated. Handicap accessible. Bathing suits required.

Twenty geothermally heated rooms and a picnic area are available on the premises. It is less than five blocks to all other services. Credit cards accepted. Renovations and additions are in process, call for updates.

Location: On US 89 at the west end of White Sulphur Springs.

Photo courtesy of Boulder Hot Springs

Originally designated as a sanctuary by the Native Americans and consequently called Peace Valley, the hot springs lies at the edge of Deerlodge National Forest, home to an amazing array of wildlife.

605   BOULDER HOT SPRINGS BED AND BREAKFAST

■

PO Box 930   406 225-4339
Boulder, MT 59632
www.boulderhotsprings.com

Large historic resort built in 1888 is carefully being restored to its former charm. Nestled in the heart of Montana's Peace Valley, it was the first permanent building in the area. It is on 274 acres at the edge of Deerlodge National Forest and was designated by the Indians as a sanctuary where fighting was not permitted. Elevation 5,000 feet. Open all year on a day-use fee basis. Call for hours.

Natural mineral water, pure enough to drink, flows out of several springs at temperatures between 150° and 175° and is piped to indoor and outdoor pools where it is cooled with water from the cold spring. Three newly tiled indoor pools with changing and shower area, offer men and women separate facilities for soaking. The women's bathhouse offers one hot pool maintained at 104° and a cooler one at 68°, while the men's bathhouse has one hot pool at 104°. All indoor pools are large enough for at least thirty people. Water continually flows through, every four hours, and all pools are completely drained and filled on a regular basis. There are saunas in both bathhouses, and bathing suits are optional. Pools are handicap accessible with some assistance.

The outdoor swimming pool is treated with bromine, and water temperatures range from 92-99°, depending on season. Bathing suits are required. All pools are handicap accessible with assistance.

Soaking is included with the overnight accommodations, seven out of the twelve available rooms include breakfast. Rooms are available for seminars, workshops, and retreats. Breakfast is served daily and Sunday Brunch has become popular with the locals. Several rooms are wheelchair accessible. Nearby attractions include plenty of hiking, skiing, fishing, panoramic views, Elkhorn Ghost Town, Lewis and Clark Caverns State Park, and the Radon Mines, known for their therapeutic qualities. Other services are available in nearby Boulder, Butte, or Helena. No pets or alcohol are allowed on the premises. Smoking outdoors only. Credit cards accepted.

Boulder Hot Springs is approximately 3.6 miles south of I-15 on MT 69. Airport pickup can be arranged. Phone for rates, reservations, and directions.

Photos above and below by Chris Andrews

606   RENOVA HOT SPRINGS

● **South of the town of Whitehall**

Small soaking pool along the Jefferson River. Open all year; springs are under water when the river runs too high and are way too hot when the river is too low.

Camping available. All other services are back in Whitehall.

Directions: From the junction of MT 2 and MT 55 (on the west side of Whitehall) drive south on MT 55 for 9.6 miles. Turn left on Rt. 422 towards Waterloo Dr. 0.6 miles and turn left on a good gravel road. Drive 2.1 miles to a "T" in the road. Turn left and drive 3.4 miles to the parking area by the river. The pool is 0.2 miles further down the road on the left side.

GPS: N 45 47.466 W 112 07.620

Photos by Chris Andrews

The main pool has a continual flow-through rate of ninety gallons per minute. The nearby wood burning sauna is the perfect complement. The enclosed upper springs are for private use only.

607A   POTOSI HOT SPRINGS
■   PO Box 651   406 685-3330
      Pony, MT 59747   888 685-1695
      www.potosiresort.com

Newly constructed and well-equipped rustic log cabins and lodge on the site of an 1890s historic hotel originally built for gold miners of the area. Located in the Tobacco Root Mountains in Beaverhead National Forest. Elevation 6,200 feet. Open all year. Roads are kept plowed in winter. (No day-use.)

Geothermal, sulfur-free mineral water flows up through the ground and emerges from granite cliffs directly into the large outdoor recreational pool where there is continual flow-through so that no chemicals are necessary. The twenty- by sixty-foot pool is maintained at 92°. The nearby wood burning sauna is the perfect complement. The pool is drained and scrubbed every two weeks, or more frequently if needed.

The Spring House, a private indoor soaking pool, contains a rock pool that dates back to the 1890s. Water from a separate spring flows in by gravity at 102°, with a shut-off valve for draining and cleaning. Lanterns and candles are provided. During the day sunlight streams in through a picturesque stainglass window.

Part of the runoff from the pools goes into the creek; and part is channeled through pipes into the lodge and cabins for heating. Spring water is used for drinking and showers. Pools are handicap accessible, with assistance.

Management has an open policy about bathing suit requirements, leaving it up to the consensus of the bathers. Pools and facilities are available to registered guests only.

Facilities include a sauna near the pools, a lodge, and creek-front cabins that sleep up to six in each. One cabin is wheelchair accessible. Potosi serves organic gourmet cuisine for all three meals either on the American Plan or a la carte. Massage is available. Gas, grocery store, and other services are twelve miles away in Harrison. Summer and winter outdoor activities are readily available on site and in the surrounding area. Reservations can be made through the resort. Major credit cards and personal checks accepted.

Phone for rates, reservations, and directions.

Photos by Chris Andrews

607B   NUPOTOSI HOT SPRINGS

● **South of the town of Pony**

Two small soaking pools in a beautiful valley in the Beaverhead National Forest with a clear view of the Tobacco Root Mountains. Elevation 6,600 feet. Open all year based on road conditions.

Natural mineral water flows directly up from the sides and bottom to fill the two rock-and-sand pools. The first pool, approximately nine- by six-feet is 101-106°. The second pool, seven feet in diameter is 98-103°. Bathing suits are optional although the pools are very popular in the summer and on weekends, and you may need to negotiate.

There are no services on the premises. It is about three-quarters of a mile to the Potosi Campground at the trailhead, and nine miles to all other services in Pony.

Directions: From the east end of Pony (consider this mile 0) take S. Willow Creek Rd 3.1 miles to a "T". Turn right (this is still called S. Willow Creek Rd.) and travel southwest. At mile point 6.7 the Potosi Lodge is on the right. Continue past the lodge to the campground at 8.6 miles. Take the first campground entrance, pass the entry into the campground itself and proceed 0.2 miles to a turnaround, the trailhead. From the trailhead follow the well-worn trail to a fence.

Nupotosi is a rarity in Montana–a natural hot spring you can actually soak in. It is adjacent to private property and you must close a gate to get to it. Please do so, and also pack out what you pack in. Let's not lose this one.

Go through the gate, making sure to close it. Continue north along the edge of the private property. The trail roughly follows the fence line 0.75 miles through pines and meadows to the spring. The spring is surrounded by a pole fence, 10-12 meters below the trail.

Source map: *Beaverhead Deerlodge National Forest* (springs not listed).

GPS: N 45 35.100   W 111 53.802

608 ELKHORN HOT SPRINGS
PO Box 460514   800 722-8978
Polaris, MT 59746
www.elkhornhotsprings.com

Mountain resort, rustic lodge and cabins situated among the tall trees of Beaverhead National Forest. Elevation 7,300 feet. Open all year.

Natural mineral water flows out of six springs with temperatures ranging from 106-120°. The outdoor swimming pool is maintained at 88-95° and the outdoor soaking pool at 95-104°. There is one coed Roman sauna maintained at 105-108°. All pools are drained and refilled weekly. Pools and west sauna are available to the public as well as to registered guests. Some areas are handicap accessible. Bathing suits required.

Dressing rooms, restaurant, tent spaces, picnic area, RV spaces, overnight camping, and cabins are available on the premises. Horseback riding, backpacking, hunting, fishing, rock and mineral hunting, skiing, and snowmobile trails are available nearby. Cross-country ski rental is available on the premises. Pick-up service is provided from the city of Butte by prior arrangement. Credit cards accepted.

Directions: Elkhorn Hot Springs is 43 miles northwest of Dillon, and 65 miles southwest of Butte. From I-15 three miles south of Dillon, take MT 278 west 25 miles to the large sign for Maverick Mt. Ski Area, Polaris, etc. Turn north and follow the Pioneer Scenic Byway 14 miles to the resort.

Photos by Chris Andrews

Jackson Hot Springs was discovered by Lewis and Clark in 1806 and mentioned in Clark's journal. Jackson is surrounded by several mountain ranges with numerous streams and high mountain lakes. Wildlife, including golden and bald eagles, is abundant.

609 JACKSON HOT SPRINGS
PO Box 808   406 834-3151
Jackson, MT 59736
www.jacksonhotsprings.com

Renovated lodge and cabins on the main street of a small town. Log construction, knotty pine interiors, and a massive stone fireplace in the main lodge add to the rustic warmth and western charm. Elevation 6,400 feet. Open all year.

Natural mineral water flows out of a spring at 137° and is piped to cabins and a large thirty- by seventy-five-foot outdoor pool. The temperature in the pool is maintained at 98-100° and operates on a flow-through basis. Water temperatures in cabin bathtubs can be controlled by adding cold tap water as needed. The swimming pool is available to the public as well as to registered guests. Bathing suits are required.

Facilities include dressing rooms, lodge complex with 16 cabins, a full-service restaurant, large western-style bar, and dance hall. Overnight camping and RV hookups are available on the premises. It is one block to a store and service station. Visa and MasterCard are accepted.

Location: On MT 278 on the main street in the town of Jackson. 140 miles southwest of Missoula.

610 FAIRMONT HOT SPRINGS RESORT

1500 Fairmont Rd   406 797-3241
Anaconda, MT 59711   800 332-3272
www.FairmontMontana.com

A five-hundred acre, full service resort cradled by the Continental Divide. Elevation 5,300. Open all year.

Natural mineral water flows out of a spring at 160° and is piped to a 350-foot enclosed water slide and a group of pools, where it is treated with chlorine. The indoor and outdoor swimming pools are maintained at 88-94° and the indoor and outdoor soaking pools range from 100-104°. There are also men's and women's steam rooms. Facilities are available to the public as well as to registered guests. Pool area is wheel chair accessible, as are specially equipped guest rooms. Bathing suits required.

Locker rooms, two restaurants, lounge, rooms, mini-zoo, tennis, golf course, are available on the premises. Overnight camping, RV hookups, country store, and gas station are nearby. Fishing, snowmobiling, hunting, horse-back riding, and skiing are all close by. All major credit cards accepted. For further information go to the web site or send an email to fairmontmt@aol.com.

Directions: From I-90 15 miles west of Butte, take the Gregson-Fairmont exit (#211) and follow signs to the resort.

Fairmont Hot Springs: A 350-foot enclosed water slide, along with a mini-zoo, makes the Fairmont a popular destination resort for families with children. Adults can entertain themselves with golf, tennis, and a video casino right on the premises.

Courtesy of Fairmont Hot Springs Resort

611   NIMROD SPRINGS

●   **East of the town of Clinton**

A popular warm swimming hole along the north side of I 90 with an underground room accessible only by the adventurous. Located at the base of the Garnet Mountains. Elevation 3,600 feet. Open all year.

Natural mineral water around 70° flows over the edge of a cliff into a large pool, eight-feet deep in places. Warmer water comes in from the bottom of the pond around the huge boulder that protrudes into the pond. In the summer, a small room inside the cliff is accessible by swimming under the water to get into the room. A suit seems preferred based on the proximity to the road, but it is not uncommon to encounter skinnydippers.

There are no services on the premises. It is approximately seven miles to Beaver Tail Hill Campground, and all other services can be found either in Bearmouth, seven miles away, or in Clinton, fifteen miles away.

Directions: From Clinton, travel east and take the Bearmouth exit north off of I-90. Three/quarters of a mile to the north, the road "Ts." Turn left for another 0.5 mile until it ends. The spring is on the north side of I 90 at milemarker 136.7. Continue walking another 0.5 mile, sometimes along the interstate, around a big cut, crossing a small creek, until you see the waterfall. It is located in the middle of a large "S" bend. Parking is a problem and the authorities suggest you not park within the "S". Instead, park along the interstate, making sure you are completely off the shoulder and not blocking traffic. You may need to park as far as 0.5 miles away. There are signs near the springs prohibiting parking.

Sources Maps: *Lolo National Forest;* USGS *Bearmouth* (springs not listed on either map).

GPS: N 46 42.318 W 113 27.378

Summertime! The weather is hot, but this large swimming hole offers a refreshing waterfall and soak. For those of you brave souls there is also a room inside this cave which can only be reached by swimming under water.

Known in previous times as Gallogly Springs, this resort has a colorful history. For years it was a secluded stopping place for travelers crossing the Continental Divide at the pass. The old Indian trail climbs about 2,000 feet in three miles, making it a very difficult trek. People would often stop to rest at the springs before starting the long climb. Later, farmers taking their produce to market would stop at the springs for the night. Nowadays, home-style cooking and a natural mineral water pool make it a great destination resort.

612 LOST TRAILS HOT SPRINGS RESORT

8321 Hwy 93 S	406 821-3574
Sula, MT 59871	800 825-3574

www.losttrailhotsprings.com

Historic rustic mountain resort, located on beautifully forested private land within the Bitterroot National Forest. Elevation 5,000 feet. Open all year. Call ahead in winter when pools may be closed Monday and Tuesday.

Natural mineral water bubbles up at 108-110° and flows by gravity through pipes at 100 gallons per minute to a large twenty-one- by seventy-foot outdoor swimming pool. Runoff is diverted to the creek below. Inflow pipes are laid under the concrete surrounding the pools so they don't ice up in winter. There is an adjoining ten-inch deep, ten- by twenty-one-foot kiddy pool. The pools are covered by a dome in winter, keeping the air temperature warm enough to grow bananas or oranges.

Indoors is a sauna and a fiberglass hot tub in a separate wood-paneled room. The water temperature is maintained at 106°. Pools and sauna are available on a day-use basis.

Facilities include dressing rooms, rustic housekeeping cabins, a motel, two lodges which can accommodate large groups and family reunions of up to thirty people, full bar with casino, restaurant, fireplace, children's play area, and a convenience store. There are also RV spaces with hookups. A National Forest campground is two-tenths of a mile north of the resort.

Activities in the surrounding wilderness area include hiking, alpine and Nordic skiing, fishing, backpacking, horseback riding, and rafting. It is six miles to a post office/general store in Sula and twenty-five miles to all other services in Darby. Most major credit cards accepted.

Location: On Hwy 93, 6 miles south of Sula, Montana, 6 miles north of the Montana-Idaho border at Lost Trails Pass. The resort is 88 miles south of Missoula, Montana and 55 miles north of Salmon, Idaho.

Bob Seal

Jayson Loam

613   LOLO HOT SPRINGS RESORT

■
38500 Highway 12   406 273-2290
Lolo, MT 59847   800 273-2290
www.lolohotsprings.net

An historic resort that has been restored and expanded, nestled in the heart of the Lolo National Forest near the Selway-Bitterroot Wilderness, 30 miles west of Missoula. Elevation 4,700 feet. Open all year.

Natural mineral water flows out of several springs at temperatures ranging from 110°-117° and is piped to two pools that are built directly over the springs themselves. Water is pumped up into the pools, and with continual flow-through the water in each pool is completely exchanged every twenty-four hours, requiring only minimal chlorination. The large outdoor pool maintains a temperature of 75-98°, weather depending. The indoor covered soaking pool maintains a temperature of 103-105° and is drained and cleaned nightly. Bathing suits required.

Facilities include dressing rooms, bathhouse, seasonal RV park, campground, tepees for rent, and a picnic area. Full-service restaurant; saloon with casino, mini-gift shop, and newly built rustic log motel (406 273-2201) are available on the premises. Most facilities are open year-round. Recreational activities include hiking, mountain biking, horseback riding, snowmobiling, and cross-country skiing. Snowmobile rental are available from the lodge. Call during heavy snow regarding status of RV park and campgrounds. Credit cards accepted. All other services are available twenty-five miles east in Lolo. Phone for rates and reservations.

Location: On US 12, 25 miles west of Lolo, MT, 7 miles east of the Montana-Idaho border.

Quinn's Paradise Resort: Fun is the key word for this family resort where kids and their parents can soak in the separate outdoor swimming and hydrojet pools.

614   QUINN'S PARADISE RESORT:
A NATURAL HOT SPRINGS

■
PO Box 219   406 826-3150
Paradise, MT 59856

Complete family resort on the banks of the Clark Fork River. Elevation 2,700 feet. Open all year.

Natural mineral water flows out of a spring at 120°. The outdoor swimming pool is treated with chlorine and maintained at a temperature of 88°. The outdoor hydrojet pool is maintained at 100° and operates on a flow-through basis so that only minimal chemical treatment of the water is needed. There are two indoor, private-space fiberglass tubs in which the water temperature can be controlled by the customer. These pools are drained and refilled after each use, so that no chemical treatment is necessary. Pools are available to the public as well as to registered guests. Bathing suits are required except in private spaces.

Dressing rooms, cafe, bar, store, rooms and cabins, overnight camping, RV hookups, and fishing are available on the premises. It is eleven miles to the service station in Plains (on MT 200). Most major credit cards accepted.

Location: On MT 135, 3 miles south of the junction with MT 200, which is east of St. Regis.

Courtesy of Symes Hot Springs

615 SYMES HOT SPRINGS HOTEL AND MINERAL BATHS

PO Box 651   406 741-2361

209 Wall St.   888 305-3106

Hot Springs, MT 59845

www.symeshotsprings.com

Historic, recently restored hotel with a long tradition of hot mineral water baths and comfortable lodgings. Elevation 2,900 feet. Open all year.

Natural mineral water flows out of an artesian well at 108° and is piped directly to the outdoor tubs, then heated as needed for use in the indoor soaking tubs to temperatures of 105-107°. There are four individual soaking tubs in the coed bathhouse. Temperature is controllable within each tub, and no chemical treatment is added. The hot water, at temperatures between 102-104°, also fills the outdoor twelve-foot octagon pool that spills into a lower twenty-foot square lower pool and into a new twenty by forty-foot warm water swimming pool. For those extra hot summer days there is also a cold pool. Minimal chlorination is required. For romance, try the two-person private tub with and steam room. Soaks are available to the public for a fee, as well as to registered guests. Mineral water is piped to many of the hotel rooms. Bathing suits required in public areas.

There are shower rooms, thirty-one hotel rooms (ten with mineral water), and a new, deluxe hot tub suite with a six-person tub, a full sauna, and kitchenette, that will sleep four. An antique shop, espresso bar, an art studio, kitchen facilities, a small conference room and a large, new event hall, hair salon and bike rentals can also be found at the hotel. Massage and Watsu therapy are also available. There is a full service restaurant on the premises, and a cafe, store, and service station are within two blocks. Credit cards accepted.

Directions: From MT 382 northeast of St. Regis, follow signs to the town of Hot Springs and then to the hotel.

You can still enjoy a soak in a claw-footed bathtub from 1928 when the hotel was built, or enjoy these new mineral water outdoor pools. As a special treat an open-air concert is offered at the resort every Friday and Saturday night presented by the Hot Springs Artist's Society.

Photos by Chris Andrews

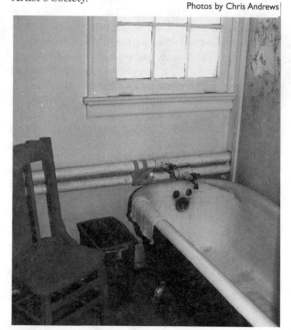

616   CAMAS SPRINGS

■   **North side of the town of Hot Springs**

Two locations for soakers and travelers alike located east of the old bath house on the Flathead Indian Reservation. Elevation 3500 feet. Open all year. Fee charged.

Big Medicine Soak: Natural mineral water comes out of ground at 120° and is piped to an eight by twenty-foot concrete pool offering a soothing soak in 102-104° water. It also fills a smaller, cooler pool. The mud bath area has benches to lie on and a hot water hose to clean you off and the area around you. The pools would be handicap accessible with assistance. Bathing suits are required.

There is also a picnic area, barbeque, and RV parking and RV sites with hookups at an additional fee.

Rose's Recreation Center, Plunge and RV Park: Natural mineral water comes out of ground at 116° and fills an eight by twenty-foot concrete pool offering a relaxing soak in 102-104° water.

The recreation center offers massage, food and beverages as well as a place to work out, or simply take a shower. RV parking and RV sites with hookups at an additional fee.

All other services are within a short distance in the town of Hot Springs.

Originally these were the source pools for the old Camas tribal bathhouse which closed around 1990. Currently the land and water is provided by the Confederated Salish and Kootenai Tribes and Camas Springs.

Photos by Robin Swan
Mud bath photo by Chris Andrews

617   **WILD HORSE HOT SPRINGS**
       PO Box 629   **406 741-3777**
■   **Hot Springs, MT 59845**

Well-maintained, family hot pool establishment with overnight facilities surrounded by rolling foothills. Elevation 2,750 feet. Open all year.

Natural mineral water flows out of an artesian well at 124° and is piped to the bathhouse building. There are six large indoor soaking pools in private rooms, each with steam bath, sauna, shower, and toilet. Pool water temperature is controllable by each customer up to 110°. The pools are scrubbed down frequently, so no chemical treatment is needed. Bathing suits are not required in private rooms.

Two motel rooms, a picnic area, overnight camping, and RV hookups are available on the premises. Overnight accommodations include a soak. Geothermal heat is used in all buildings. It is six miles to all other services. Enlargement of the facilities is in the plans—call for status of construction. No credit cards accepted.

Directions: From MT 28, 2.5 miles north of Hot Springs junction, follow signs 2 miles east on the gravel road to the resort.

While the tubs have all been recently redone, the mud baths are still the same, and there is no charge for using them.

Jayson Loam

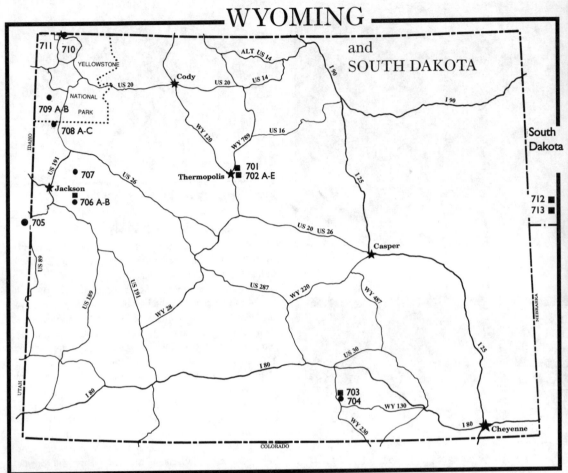

WYOMING

and
SOUTH DAKOTA

This map was designed to be used with a standard highway map.

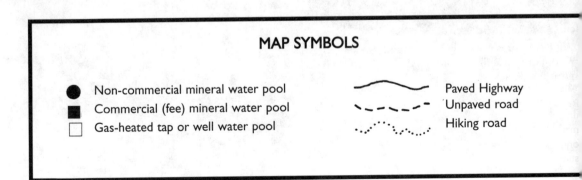

MAP SYMBOLS

● Non-commercial mineral water pool

■ Commercial (fee) mineral water pool

☐ Gas-heated tap or well water pool

〜 Paved Highway

– – – Unpaved road

⋯⋯ Hiking road

It is probable that the well that fills this 200-foot by 72-foot pool taps the same hot mineral water reservoir as that which supplies the Big Spring in Thermopolis. The water flow is so enormous that the pool water is exchanged every 11 hours. The well was originally drilled in 1918 in a search for oil. Instead, hot mineral water came gushing out under such pressure that the derrick was destroyed.

701   FOUNTAIN OF YOUTH RV PARK
       PO Box 711   307 864-3265
■   Thermopolis, WY 82443
       www.trib.com/~foyrvpk/

Well-kept RV park featuring a unique, huge soaking pool fed by an artesian well. Elevation 3,900 feet. Open March 1 to October 31.

Natural mineral water at 130° flows out of the historic Sacajawea Well at the rate of over one million gallons per day. The well itself looks like a small volcano. Water is channeled through a cooling pond into a 200-foot-long soaking pool where the temperature varies from 104° at the warm end down to 99° at the outflow where it continues into the scenic Big Horn River. The pool needs no chemical treatment due to the huge volume of water that flows through each day. A special ramp makes the pool handicap accessible. The pool is available only to registered day and overnight campers. Bathing suits required.

Rest rooms, showers, picnic sites, laundry, RV supplies, overnight camping, and RV hookups are available on the premises. It is two miles to all other services. Visa and MasterCard accepted.

Location: On US 20, two miles north of the town of Thermopolis.

Photos courtesy of Fountain of Youth

The Labor Day vacation enables these families to enjoy the largest mineral pool in Wyoming and the third largest in the world.

Thermopolis, a Greek word for "Hot City," is located next to Hot Springs State Park, which offers several different places to enjoy a hot mineral soak. All of the establishments on the grounds are supplied with natural mineral water from the Big Springs. Big Horn Hot Springs releases 2.8 million gallons daily and is one of the largest mineral springs in the world.

Walkways have been provided through the large tufa terraces that have been built up by mineral deposits from the spring over the centuries. These terraces, hot waterfalls, a dinosaur museum and the state's bison herd—in addition to a nice relaxing soak—makes the trip to the park, only two hours from Yellowstone, well worthwhile.

This square mile of land was presented to the State of Wyoming by the Federal Government after it had been purchased from the Shoshone and Arapahoe Indians in 1896. Annually, in August, the Shoshone Indians set up their tepees and reenact the "Wedding of the Waters," portraying the sale of the springs.

For more information, contact the Thermopolis Chamber of Commerce, 800-SUN-N-SPA.

Courtesy of the Chamber of Commerce

702A STATE BATH HOUSE
State Park   307 864-3765
■ Thermopolis, WY 82443

The temperature in the sixteen indoor (eight men's and eight women's) individual soaking tubs is adjustable by the person using the tub. All pools use minimally chlorinated, flow-through mineral water. No charge is made for pool or tub use.

Changing rooms are available, and bathing suits are required in the outdoor communal pools where the water is kept at 104°. There is a nominal charge for renting suits or towels. No credit cards accepted.

702B TEPEE SPA
PO Box 750   307 864-9250
■ Thermopolis, WY 82443

At this commercial location, these outdoor and indoor swimming pools are maintained at 92-96° year-round, and the indoor soaking pool is maintained at 104°. The indoor steambath is maintained at 110-115°. There are three outdoor hot tubs with temperatures varying from 100-106°. There are also giant indoor and outdoor water slides, and a kiddie pool. All pools operate on a flow-through basis, so no chemicals are needed. Ramps and railings make the hot tubs handicap accessible. Bathing suits required.

A steam room, dry sauna, picnic area, locker rooms and a snack bar and gift shop are available on the premises. It is also possible to book a standard or a Watsu massage. Credit cards accepted.

A treaty between the Shoshone and Arapaho nations and the United States specified that some of the waters were to be free to all. The State Bath House (picture, left) honors this commitment.

'02C STAR PLUNGE
PO Box 627   307 864-3771
Thermopolis, WY 82443

A wide assortment of places to play in the water include an outdoor swimming pool maintained at 92-96°, in indoor swimming pool maintained at 94-98°, one indoor and one outdoor hot tub at 104°, three jacuzzi tubs with super bubble jets, three water slides (one inside, one outside, and the Super Star Plunge), several baby pools, and a vapor cave at 118°. All pools are flow-through with a complete turnover every six to eight hours, requiring no chemical treatment. Handicap accessible areas. Bathing suits required.

Locker rooms and a snack bar are available on the premises. No credit cards accepted (personal checks okay).

Super Star 500 Ft. water slide at the STAR PLUNGE

Butch Cassidy and the Hole in the Wall gang made this their watering stop. Given their sense of adventure, they would have really enjoyed the water slides.

'02D PLAZA HOTEL/QUALITY INN
116 East Park St.   888 919-9009
Thermopolis, WY 82443
www.bestofwyoming.com

Located on the banks of the beautiful Big Horn River, the Plaza Hotel, originally built in 1918, has been completely remodeled. The thirty-six room hotel (eighteen of the rooms are suites), are furnished with lodgepole furniture in a romantic decor. Upstairs rooms have fireplaces.

Continental breakfast is included with all rooms. Two suites are handicap accessible.

Two outside hot tubs, kept at 104°, will hold about twelve people each. No chemicals are required. During the summer, regular tap water fills the swimming pool.

Note: Their web site is one of the best if you are interested in what else there is to do in this area.

702E HOLIDAY INN
PO Box 1323   307 864-3131
■ Thermopolis, WY 82443
holinn@trib.com

Major hotel with a unique adaptation of men's and women's bathhouses. Each bathhouse has private spaces for four individual soaking tubs, two saunas and two steambaths. The private spaces are rented to couples, even though they are in the men's and women's bathhouses.

The Big Spring Spa offers private soaking tubs, a steam room, and a private hydrojet room, all of which use natural mineral water, and are drained after each use so that no chemical treatment is needed. The outdoor hydrojet pool also uses natural mineral water and is maintained at a temperature of 104°. The outdoor swimming pool uses gas-heated, chlorine-treated tap water and is maintained at a temperature of 81-84°. There is also a private indoor hydropool. All pools and the athletic club facilities are available to the public as well as to registered guests. Hotel is fully handicap accessible. Bathing suits required in all outdoor public areas.

Restaurant and hotel rooms are available on the premises. All season sports and equipment rentals are available at the inn or close by. Major credit cards accepted.

Courtesy of Holiday Inn

Present-day explorers have the advantage of a warm, relaxing soak after a hard day fishing or hunting, as did the early settlers to this area.

703 THE SARATOGA INN, A HOT SPRINGS SPA

601 E Pic Pike Rd.   307 326-5261
Saratoga, WY 82331   800 594-0178
www.saratogainn.com

Located along the pristine North Platte River, the Inn boasts one of the Rocky Mountains' most beautiful sites with a challenging nine hole golf course, mountain lake and stream fishing, as well as guided river fishing, scenic river float tours, unforgettable Sierra Madre horseback rides, snowmobiling, cross country skiing and hot mineral water pools.

Hot mineral baths are located right outside your lodge room with three special, tepee covered baths for private soaking, with temperatures ranging from 105-112°. A twenty-three yard mineral spring swimming pool is located off the five soaking pools and is kept at 100°, with chlorine added as needed. Pool use is reserved for registered guests. Pools are handicap accessible with ramps. Bathing suits are required.

The Inn offers an enticing menu selected by their certified executive chef, a micro-brewery offering hand-crafted beers brewed on-site, and the Healing Waters Spa, offering full, luxurious body treatments and massage. Corporate retreats are a specialty in these unique surroundings. Credit cards accepted.

Location: Off of Wyoming Rt 130, a National Scenic Byway, on one of the "ten best road tour drives in the US," Saratoga is only three and one-half hours from Denver, one hour from Laramie and two hours from Cheyenne. A corporate-jet airport is located one mile south of the resort.

For a private soak, try one of the hot spring poo● inside one of the tepees. Follow this treat by a relaxin● body treatment in the Healing Waters Spa.

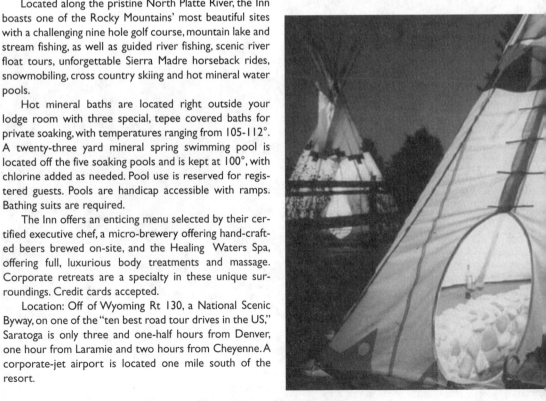

Hobo Pool: Thanks to the town council, there's not only a fenced swimming pool which charges a fee, but a large soaking pool that is free to everyone.

704 HOBO POOL

In the town of Saratoga

An improved but unfenced soaking pool, newly enhanced with a wall of moss rock, and a fenced municipal swimming pool located on the banks of the North Platte River. Elevation 6,800 feet. Open all year.

Natural mineral water flows out of the source spring at 115°. A large cement soaking pool (free to the public) maintains a temperature of 100-110°. Volunteers have channeled the soaking pool runoff into shallow rock pools along the edge of the river. A daily charge is made for the use of the swimming pool, which is maintained at 90° and is closed in the winter. Bathing suits are required.

There are showers, changing rooms, and public rest rooms on the premises. It is three blocks to all services. No credit cards are accepted.

Directions: On WY 130 in the town of Saratoga, watch for the HOBO POOL sign, then follow the signs four blocks east to the pool.

705 ALPINE WARM SPRING

(see map)

● **West of the town of Alpine**

Single, large pool located on a flat area on the south edge of Palisades Reservoir, one-hundred feet down from the high water mark. Elevation 5,600 feet. Only accessible very late in the season when the reservoir is low or during years with very little rainfall.

Natural mineral water bubbles up from the bottom into an eight by twelve-foot oval pool dug out of the earth at a comfortably warm 105°. Clothing optional.

Mc Coy Creek campground is three-quarters of a mile away at the trailhead and all other services are twelve miles away in Alpine.

Directions: Beginning at Alpine Junction in Alpine, Wyoming travel south on US 89 approximately 4 miles to McCoy Creek Rd. (FR 087). Turn right (west) and drive about 6 miles to the bridge over McCoy Creek. Park here and follow the edge of the reservoir approximately 0.75 miles north to the spring.

Source map: USGS *Alpine* (7.5 minute).

GPS: N 43 12.102 W 111 06.444

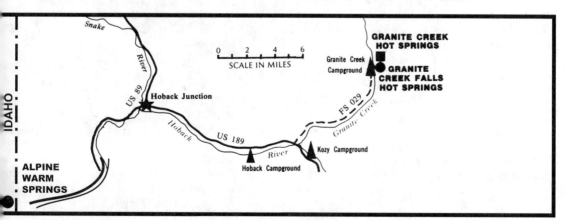

Chris Andrew

706A GRANITE CREEK HOT SPRINGS
(see map on page ▦)
183

■ **East of Hoback Junction**

Part of a major bonanza for lovers of natural beauty and natural mineral water. Elevation 7,000 feet. Open almost all year, including the winter season for those who have snow cats. Closed during the time when snow turns to slush, often for as long as two months. Check in town before heading out, or with the Bridger-Teton National Forest 307 739-5500.

Natural mineral water flows out of a spring at 112° and tumbles directly into a large cement pool built by the CCC in the 1930s. Cold stream water is added as needed to maintain the pool temperature of 95° in the summer and 105° in the winter. The pool is drained and refilled each day, so no chemical treatment is needed. Bathing suits are required.

Changing rooms and rest rooms are available on the premises, which are operated under a lease with the Forest Service. Suits and towels are for rent. The site is closed and gates are locked at 8 PM or one hour before dark. A day-use fee is charged. There is a picnic area with firepits near the pool and Granite Creek Campground, a large, wooded, creekside campground is 0.5 miles away. Primitive camping is available on open stretches at creekside along the ten-mile gravel road between the highway and the springs. It is eighteen miles to a cafe and motel and twenty-two miles to all other services.

Directions: From Jackson, drive 13 miles south on U 191/189 to Hoback Junction. Bear left and continue 11. miles on US 191/189 to Granite Creek Road. Turn lef (consider this point 0). Bear right at 1.4 miles an continue 8 miles into the parking area.

Marjorie Youn

Granite Creek Hot Springs was built by the Civilia Conservation Corps (CCC) in 1933 and is currentl operated under a special-use permit granted by the Bridger-Teton National Forest.

Photos by Chris Andrews

06B GRANITE CREEK FALLS HOT SPRINGS (see map on page 183)
East of Hoback Junction

A series of primitive rock-and-sand soaking pools are located along the creek at the foot of Granite Creek Falls. A small waterfall at 118° seeps up from underground and flows down a creek bank adjacent to Granite Falls and into a series of volunteer-built pools where temperatures range from 96-110°. Temperature can be controlled by diverting the water or by mixing it with cold creek water. These pools must be rebuilt after each annual high-water washout. Although the spring is partly visible from the road, the apparent local custom is clothing optional. However, in popular summer months bathing suits seem to be preferred.

Several trails lead to these primitive pools. From the fee-area concrete pool, a trail leads off to the left just before the bridge over the creek. It is a ten to fifteen minute walk along this narrow trail to a spot above the falls where a steep trail heads off to the right down to the creek where volunteers rebuild a variety of pools each year. These pools can also be reached from the parking area for Granite Falls, which is approximately ten miles in from the main highway and one-quarter mile before the fee-area pool. To reach the pools, it is necessary to ford the very swiftly flowing creek. Do not attempt to ford the creek during high water. A third trail leads up from the Girl Scout Camp parking and trailhead area, which is eight miles in from the highway along the gravel road, before the falls.

Directions: From Jackson, drive 13 miles south on US 191/189 to Hoback Junction. Bear left and continue 11.4 miles on US 191/189 to Granite Creek Road. Turn left (consider this point 0). Bear right at 1.4 miles. At 8.7 miles turn right and drive towards the falls. Park in the parking loop, cross the creek and walk to the pools at the base of the falls.

There is also a trail from the Granite Creek Hot Springs pool.

Source map: USGS *Granite Falls*.
GPS: N 43 21.906 W 110 26.646

Chris Andrew

Whether there are patches of snow on the hills surrounding the pool and the Grand Tetons, or the pool surrounded by summer wildflowers, people enjoy soaking here all year except in severe winter months.

707   KELLY WARM SPRINGS

● **Northeast of Jackson**

Large warm pond with a gorgeous view of the Grand Tetons, located within the national park. Wonderful for a summer soak. Elevation 6,700 feet. Open all year except for the worst part of winter.

Natural mineral water flows directly into a large gravel-bottom pool up to eight feet deep in an open meadow. The water temperature of 81° makes this an ideal hot-weather soak, albeit a bit cool in winter. The pool is adjacent to the road, so bathing suits are advisable.

There are no services available on the premises. The nearest campground, Gros Ventre, is five miles away in Grand Teton National Park. All other services are twenty miles away in Jackson.

Directions: From Jackson, drive north on US 189/191 about 7 miles to Gros Ventre Junction. Turn right on Gros Ventre Road (consider this point 0). Drive through the town of Kelly following the left curve which comes up at about 7 miles. At 8.2 miles you will come to Gros Ventre Rd. Turn right (east). The springs are 0.4 of a mile and are clearly visible from the road.

Source maps: USGS *Shadow Mountain. Bridger Teton National Forest.*

GPS: N 43 38.382 W 110 36.960

HUCKLEBERRY HOT SPRINGS

The springs were originally developed as a commercial swimming area in the 1960s and continued to operate, free of charge, until the pool was closed by the Park Service in 1983 to let the area return to its natural state. This action included bulldozing the swimming pool and removing the access bridge over Polecat Creek. Now it is necessary to wade Polecat Creek in order to get to the springs from the parking area at the end of the old access road. Trails in the area are not maintained.

See full description of Huckleberry on page 188.

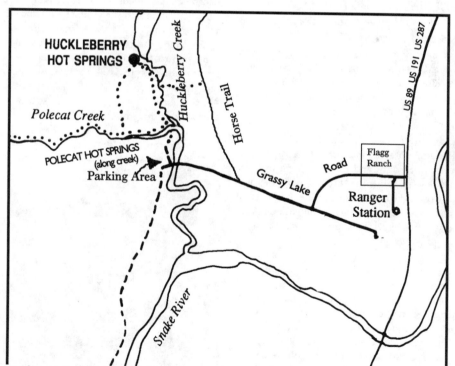

Chris Andrews

You need to go through Flagg Ranch to access Grassy Lake Road. An alternate path to the springs in case Polecat Creek is too high to cross near the parking area is to go back and take the obvious horse trail along the ridge above the creek. Walk for about fifteen minutes and turn left on a well-worn foot path. Continue another ten minutes to reach the pools.

708A   HUCKLEBERRY HOT SPRINGS
(see map on previous page)
● **North of the town of Jackson**

Large group of primitive hot springs along the north bank of Polecat Creek within the John D. Rockerfeller, Jr. Memorial Parkway, near the south entrance to Yellowstone National Park. Elevation 6,800 feet. Open all year.

Natural mineral water flows out of many springs at temperatures up to 130°, cooling as it follows various channels to the creek. The hottest and most spectacular flow is where hot water bubbles up into a large pond, flows over hot lava rocks, and tumbles down in a hot waterfall into a soaking pool at 110°. Runoff goes into Huckleberry Creek. The entire creek below this point has hot water, and volunteers have built small rock-and-mud soaking pools at several places where the water is in the 100-105° range. Although this is close to Yellowstone, there are very few visitors, so the apparent local custom is clothing optional. It is advisable to have a bathing suit handy in case anyone objects to skinny-dippers.

There are no services available on the premises. There is a commercial campground within one mile, and all other services are available at Flagg Ranch, 1.25 miles away. Flagg Ranch, a private operation, does allow the Park Service to have a Visitors Information office on the premises where some information is provided on the springs and camping areas. Primitive camping areas are also available along Grassy Lake Road, past the turnoff for the springs.

Directions: Access Grassy Lake Road through Flagg Ranch Village. Immediately after crossing a bridge look for a parking pullout on the right. The trail begins here as an abandoned road. It is a short five-minute walk to Polecat Creek. Wade the creek and continue straight ahead for another 5 to 10 minutes. (See map for alternate route if creek is too high to wade across.) At a flat grassy area one trail veers off to the right, leading to the hot creek. Another leads straight ahead to a flat area where water seeps out of the ground just above the scalding waterfall.

Source map: USGS *Flagg Ranch*; Bridger-Teton National Forest Map (shows springs, but not trails). (Hot springs not shown on Grand Teton National Park map.)

GPS: N 44 06.894 W 110 41.220

Photos by Chris Andrews

708B-C POLECAT HOT SPRINGS
(see Huckleberry map)
North of the town of Jackson

Two groups of primitive log-and-rock soaking pools along Polecat Creek, near Huckleberry Creek and hot springs, with spectacular mountain views.

Directions: Driving and access are the same as for Huckleberry Hot Springs. From the parking area, follow the trail to Polecat Creek. After wading the creek, make an immediate left onto a trail which parallels Polecat Creek. It is a short five minute walk to the first group of pools at Lower Polecat.

B: Lower Polecat. A lovely, elaborately elevated log-and-rock soaking pool which is deep enough to sit in and large enough for eight-to-ten people stretched out. Water tumbles through the logs into the pool along the creek where, after mixing with the cool creek water, the soaking temperature is approximately 100°.

Upper Polecat: The marshy grasslands make this a difficult walk during wet weather. However, chances are good you will have the place to yourself.

C: Upper Polecat. Continue up the trail along the creek for another 15-20 minutes until the trail disappears in a large stand of pine tress. From here, Polecat Creek makes a sweeping curve to the left. Up ahead you will notice a few single pine trees at the creek's edge. Keep your eye on these. The hot pools are at the creek in this area. Walk through the stand of pines, over marshy grassland where the trail virtually disappears, and work your way toward the pine trees along the creek to the pools. (The area is very marshy and difficult to get to in the wet weather.) Hot water seeps out in two separate streams and flows into volunteer-built rock-and-log pools of varying sizes and temperatures as the hot water mixes with cool creek water. (One soaker suggested a stiff brush to clean some of the algae off the rocks.)

GPS: N 44 06.732 W 110 42.168 (Upper)
GPS: N 44 06.654 W 110 41.460 (Lower)

BECHLER RIVER AREA
In Yellowstone National Park

Boiling hot natural mineral water erupts from geyser cones and bubbles out of hot springs flowing to join nearby cold streams. Where the hot water dumps into cold creeks and rivers is the only legal place to put your body into Yellowstone's hot water. It is also the logical place to soak as the water in most other areas is way too hot.

Photos by Chris Andrews

Pack your camping gear, obtain a permit and be prepared to view magnificent *Dunanda Falls* and to soak in one of the adjacent hot pools.

709A   DUNANDA FALLS HOT SPRINGS

● **In Yellowstone National Park**

Several small pools located below the 110-foot Dunanda Falls in a beautifully forested gorge within the Bechler River area. Elevation 6,500 feet. Access depends on snowpack and spring runoff; could be late June to November.

Natural mineral water flows out of springs adjacent to the river below the falls. The 150° water flows through channels into several rock-and-sand pools at the river's edge, where the temperature can be controlled by mixing with the cold river water. The size and shape of the pools change frequently depending on the degree of flow. The apparent local custom is clothing optional.

There are no services at this location. However, there are several campgrounds throughout the Bechler River Canyon area for which camping permits are required. The springs are adjacent to a primitive campground. Cave Falls Campground is eight miles away. All other services are located twenty-five miles from the trailhead in Ashton Idaho.

If you do not already have hiking guides and/or detailed maps of the area, obtain them when you apply for a camping permit. At that time, also ask about weather conditions and any other pertinent information.

Directions: From Ashton, Idaho (ID 20), drive east on Highway 47 and follow the signs 25 miles to the Bechler Ranger Station. This is the trail head for the relatively flat 8.5 mile hike to Dunanda Falls.

GPS: N 44 14.832 W 111 01.434

709B   FERRIS FORK POOL

● **In Yellowstone National Park**

Considered by many to be the "ultimate in hot springs," these multiple rock pools are located half-way between Old Faithful and the trailhead at Bechler River Ranger Station, one-half mile south of the main trail on a marked spur trail.

Natural mineral water at temperatures up to 190° discharges into the cold water of Ferris Creek. A pleasant soak for two to three people is possible behind the rocks and logs. Two other similar locations exist nearby. One is a pool on a small side stream just below (south) of the main pool; the other is on Ferris Creek, just upstream from the main pool. The apparent local custom is clothing optional.

Maps and directions are available from the Ranger Station, and a wilderness permit is required for this easy sixteen-mile one-way hike. There are nearby wilderness campgrounds for which a permit is also required.

GPS: N 44 17.238   W 110 52.728

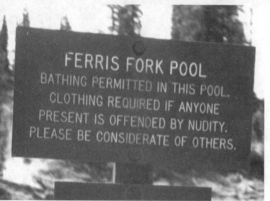

FERRIS FORK POOL
BATHING PERMITTED IN THIS POOL.
CLOTHING REQUIRED IF ANYONE
PRESENT IS OFFENDED BY NUDITY.
PLEASE BE CONSIDERATE OF OTHERS.

Photos by Chris Andrews

Ferris Fork: The Bechler River flow reaches approximately one hundred degrees below this major spring.

MADISON CAMPGROUND WARM SPRING

● **In Yellowstone National Park**

There is no longer any access to the warm water flow in the campground.

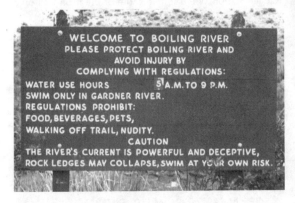

---

710   BOILING RIVER

● **In Yellowstone National Park**

Turbulent confluence of hot mineral water and cold river water along the west bank of the Gardiner River, just below Park Headquarters at Mammoth Hot Spring. Elevation 5,500 feet. Open all year during daylight hours only.

Natural mineral water flows out of a very large spring at 140° and travels thirty yards through an open channel where it tumbles down the south bank of the Gardiner River. Volunteers have rearranged rocks in the river to control the flow of cold water in an eddy pocket where the hot and cold water churn into a swirling mixture that varies from 50-110°. Bathing suits are required.

Facilities include an enclosed pit toilet at the parking area, bear-proof trash receptacles, and a bicycle rack. All other services are available in Gardner, two and one-half miles north; or refer to the NPS Yellowstone Park map for the location of all services within the park.

Directions: On the North Entrance Road, 4 miles from Mammoth Hot Spring and 2.5 miles from the town of Gardiner, look for a large parking area on both sides of the road at the Montana-Wyoming state line and the 45th Parallel sign. Turn into the parking lot behind that sign on the east side of the road, and hike 0.5 miles upstream to where Boiling River cascades over the riverbank.

Photos by Chris Andrew

711   MAMMOTH HOT SPRINGS HOTEL
      AND CABINS
      Mammoth Hot Springs   307 344-7311
❏   Yellowstone National Park, WY 82190

Four fiberglass, hydrojet pools filled with chlorinated, electrically heated tap water behind high board fences adjoining four small cabins. Elevation 6,200 feet. Call for open times.

These pools are rented for public use by the hour during the winter. During the summer they are for the private use of the registered guests in each of the four cabins. Phone for rates and reservations.

712   **EVANS PLUNGE**
       1145 North River   **605 745-5165**
■   Hot Springs, SD 57747

The world's largest natural warm water indoor swimming pool and water park, located at the north edge of the town of Hot Springs in southwestern South Dakota. Elevation 3,800 feet. Open all year.

Five thousand gallons per minute of 87° water rises out of the pebble bottom of the plunge, providing a complete change of water sixteen times daily, so only a minimum of chlorine is necessary. An outdoor pool, sauna and steam room ,large indoor and outdoor waterslides, traveling rings, fun tubes, and kiddie pools and slides are available at the plunge. Two hydrojet spas (100-104°), sauna, steam room, and fitness equipment are located in the health club. No credit cards accepted.

A gift shop is available on the premises. All other services are available within one-half mile.

Courtesy of Evans Plunge

Evans Plunge: Less than 60 miles from Mt. Rushmore the kids can find a place to play and the adults a place to relax and soak, all in natural mineral water.

El Dorado Hot Spring

Only one of the pools available for soaking.

713 SPRINGS BATH HOUSE

146 N. Garden St. 605 745-4424
Hot Springs, SD 57747 888 817-1972
www.springbathhouse.com

Springs Bath House is an historic reconstruction of the old Sulphur Bath House built in 1888, covering four acres with spring-fed indoor and outdoor pools. Historical tours are offered. Adult only environment. Open all year; hours vary with the season. Reservations recommended.

Hot mineral water is piped from the basement to several pools which include a private aromatherapy whirlpool bath and a private steam treatment chamber. The indoor soaking pool is kept at 102°, and there is a small "cool-pool" outdoors. The temperatures will vary with the seasons. Seven modalities of massage, including Swedish, deep tissue, neuromuscular, Watsu, LaStone, sports, and Rieki are offered by the best therapists available in the area. The pool, kept at body temperature, is dedicated to Watsu therapy and is the only one in the Dakotas. Two types of body wraps, a variety of body treatments, and a selection of face treatments plus body masques are all part of this "wonderland of rejuvenation." You can get an all day soak pass which includes a shower, towel, and locker. There is also a massage school and a conference center known as the "Exploratorium" located on the premises. Major credit cards accepted.

Less than a five-minute walk brings you to the downtown where you will find several fine restaurants, unique shopping, a premier museum and the Freedom Trail leading up to Kidney Springs where you can enjoy a cool drink, even fill up a jug or two for the road.

The Springs has a long-range expansion program where they plan on creating a natural setting complete with waterfalls and more pools. Call for updates.

Wind Cave National Park is twelve minutes away and Custer State Park and Mt. Rushmore, only an hour away. Evans Plunge and the Mammoth Site are within minutes of town.

Courtesy of Springs Bath House

CENTRAL, EASTERN, SOUTHERN STATES

This map was designed to be used with a standard highway map.

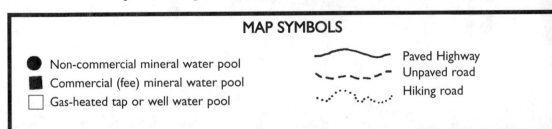

MAP SYMBOLS

● Non-commercial mineral water pool
■ Commercial (fee) mineral water pool
□ Gas-heated tap or well water pool

⌇⌇⌇ Paved Highway
- - - Unpaved road
···· Hiking road

901 SAND SPRINGS POOL

Sand Springs Road   413 458-5205
Williamstown, MA 01267

An historic seasonal plunge located in the heart of the Berkshire Hills in northwestern Massachusetts. Elevation 900 feet. Open May-September.

Natural mineral water flows out of a spring at 74° and is piped to several pools where it is gas-heated and treated with chlorine. The whirlpool is maintained at a temperature of 102°. The swimming pool and toddler's pool are maintained at approximately 80°. A grass beach for lounging is a pleasant addition. Bathing suits required.

Facilities include changing rooms, sundeck, exercise room, sauna, snack bar, dance floor, picnic tables, and large lawn. A motel, service station, restaurant and other services are available within ten blocks. No credit cards accepted.

Directions: From the Williamstown municipal building on US 7, drive north to Sand Springs Rd. Turn right and follow signs to pool.

Sand Springs Pool: This would be the perfect place for a retreat from the heat during a New England summer.

902 THE SPA

414 Mohawk Trail   413 774-2951
Greenfield, MA 01301
www.torelax.com

Beautifully situated modern spa offering a three-state view, located at the gateway to the Berkshires.

Three indoor hot tubs in beautifully redwood-panelled private rooms all with individual showers. The two outdoor tubs feature breathtaking views. The tubs are maintained at 102° and bromine treated. Four tubs are handicap accessible.

Massage, tanning rooms, a full salon, and facials are available on the premises along with lounging areas. Special "pampering" packages are available as are private party rentals. Major credit cards accepted. Phone for rates, reservations, and directions. Check web site for more details.

903 EAST HEAVEN TUB CO.

33 West St.   413 586-6843
Northampton, MA 01060
www.easthaven.com

Beautiful, Japanese-motif rental facility located on the campus of Smith College in the Connecticut Valley.

Four tubs in private spaces are located on the ground level, one outside under a roof and three inside. Three other tubs are located on the roof in private enclosures, open to the sky. Six of the tubs are teakwood. Gas-heated city water is treated with a unique combination of bromine and an ozone water filtration system that allows for a constant flow through of water. All are maintained at a temperature of 104°. Handicap accessible.

Sales of saunas, hot tubs and spas are conducted on the premises. Credit cards accepted. Phone for rates, reservations, and directions.

THE SPRINGS OF SARATOGA

The Saratoga Springs area has a two-century-old tradition of providing natural beauty, health giving geothermal water, and the gaiety of its summer racetrack season. More than a dozen springs discharge naturally carbonated mineral water along the Saratoga Fault, which is located in a low basin between Lake George and Albany.

In 1909 the state of New York created a Reservation Commission and acquired the land around Geyser Creek, which has now been designated as Saratoga Spa State Park. Some geo-thermal activities are still accessible for public viewing, such as the only spouting geyser east of the Mississippi River.

Bathing in mineral water is available only at the Lincoln mineral baths in the Park and at the Crystal Spa bathhouse in the city of Saratoga Springs. All baths have separate men's and women's sections using one-person tubs that are drained and filled after each use so that no chemical treatment of the water is necessary.

904A   LINCOLN MINERAL BATHS
518 583-2880

■   Saratoga Springs, NY 12866

Traditional mineral bath facility with nearby hotel and conference center operated by Zanterra Parks and Resorts. Open all year.

Mineral water flows out of a spring at 53° and is piped to individual tubs. Along the way it is heated to approximately body temperature.

Appointment are necessary for the following services: mineral baths, massage, reflexology, body treatments, hot stone massage, facials, manicures and pedicures. All major credit cards accepted.

Phone for rates, reservations, and directions.

904B   THE CRYSTAL SPA
120 S. Broadway   518 584-2556
■   Saratoga Springs, NY 12866
www.thecrystalspa.com

Recently constructed, privately owned spa associated with the Grand Union Motel where the mineral water is available for drinking as well as for bathing. Open all year.

Mineral water flows out of a spring at 52° and is piped to individual soaking tubs where it is mixed with 149° tap water as needed to obtain the desired soaking temperature. Separate facilities are provided for men and women.

New building additions offer expanded services. Sauna, massage, and facials, and pampering packages are available on the premises. No credit cards accepted. Be sure to phone ahead for reservations and information.

Courtesy of The Crystal Sp

The Crystal Spa: This genuine Victorian gazebo an costuming is reminiscent of ladies and gents coming t "take the waters" during the racing season.

904C   ROOSEVELT MINERAL BATHS
AND SPA

■   Saratoga Springs, NY 12866

Closed for renovation. No date set for reopening.

Courtesy of The Saratoga Spa State Park

905 BERKELEY SPRINGS STATE PARK
304 258-2711
Berkeley Springs, WV 25411
wwweb.com/www/BERKELEY-SPRINGS.html

Large, traditional bathhouse operated as a state park, located in a narrow valley in West Virginia's eastern panhandle. Elevation 620 feet. Open 361 days per year; reservations recommended.

Two thousand gallons-per-minute of mineral water flows out of several springs at a temperature of 74°. A portion of this water is steam-heated to 102° and piped to five private, one-person bathtubs in the main bathhouse and to nine private tiled baths in the Old Roman Bath House. The bathhouse is separated into men's and women's sections. All tubs are drained and refilled after each use so that no chemical treatment of the water is necessary. Each side also has a wet sauna for rent by the hour. The Old Roman Bath House is open all year. Mineral spring water is also piped directly to the outdoor swimming pool, which is treated with chlorine and is open from Memorial Day through Labor Day. Attendants are on duty to assist disabled guests. Bathing suits required in public areas.

Facilities include steam cabinets. Massage, heat treatments, and other health services are available on the premises. Visa and Mastercard are accepted. All other services are available in the adjoining town of Berkeley Springs. Phone for rates, reservations, and directions.

Courtesy of Berkeley Springs State Park

George Washington was sixteen when he first visited these springs. Later he purchased property here so that he could enjoy the waters on a regular basis.

I wonder what our founding fathers would have to say about the coed soaks at the Old Roman Bath House?

906 THE GREENBRIER

800 624-6070
304 536-1110

White Sulphur Springs, WV 24986
www.greenbrier.com

A large, historic, lavishly appointed resort occupying 6,500 acres in an upland valley of the Allegheny Mountains, near the Virginia border. A National Historic Landmark. Elevation 2,900 feet. Open all year. Acommodation prices include breakfast and dinner.

Natural mineral water flows out of a sulphur spring at 58° and is piped to individual soaking tubs in separate men's and women's sections of the the Spa and Mineral Baths, where it is heated by electricity to the desired temperature. Tubs are drained and filled after each use, so no chemical treatment is needed. Water from a fresh-water spring is piped to an outdoor pool and the Grand Indoor Pool, where it is treated with chlorine and heated by steam to a temperature of 75°. A hydraulic chair lift is available for the indoor pool. Bathing suits are required.

Facilities include 637 guest rooms and luxury suites, dining rooms and restaurants, a complete convention center, shops, service station, tennis courts, three golf courses, aerobics studio, exercise equipment, a 25,000 square foot spa and spa salon, and a complete diagnostic clinic. Services include fitness evaluations, daily exercise classes, massage, herbal wrap, facials, manicures, pedicures and full hair services. The diagnostic clinic and shops are available to the public. All other facilities are for the use of registered guests only. All major credit cards are accepted. Phone or write for rates, reservations, and directions.

The Greenbrier offers the ultimate in luxurious accommodations and facilities.

Courtesy of The Greenbrier
Dan Day, Photographer

The Homestead: The flow of water at the source spring is so great that several pools can be maintained on a flow-through basis at this 15,000 acre upscale resort.

907 THE HOMESTEAD
PO Box 2000   800 838-1766
Hot Springs, VA 24445

A very large, historic, luxurious resort on the west slope of the Allegheny Mountains near the West Virginia Border. Elevation 2,500 feet. Open all year. Room prices include breakfast and dinner.

The odorless mineral water used at the Homestead Spa flows from several springs at temperatures ranging from 102-106°. It is piped to individual, one-person bathtubs in separate men's and women's bathhouses, where it is mixed to provide an ideal temperature of 104°. Tubs are drained and refilled after each use so that no chemical treatment of the water is necessary. Mineral water from the same springs is used in an indoor swimming pool maintained at 84° and an outdoor swimming pool maintained at 72°. Both pools receive a minimum of chlorine treatment. Use of the spa and all pools is restricted to registered guests only. Bathing suits are required except as indicated in the bathhouses.

The facilities include over 500 bedrooms and parlors, world-class dining at several restaurants, redwood wine cellar, shops, conference center, bowling alley, movie theater, and tennis courts. Recreational activities available on the premises include three championship golf courses, archery, fishing, hiking, riding, skeet and trap shooting, and tennis, plus skiing and ice skating in the winter. There are many resort services available, some of which are included in the basic room rate. Phone or write for complete information. Visa, MasterCard, and American Express are accepted.

Jefferson Pools

Five miles away but still within the 15,000-acre Homestead property is the village of Warm Springs, where the water flows out of the springs at 98°. The rate of discharge is so great that the two large Warms Springs pools, in separate men's and women's buildings, maintain a temperature of 96° on a flow-through basis, requiring no chemical treatment of the water. These Warm Springs pools are open only during the warm months and are open to the public. Charge is by the hour, and no reservations are necessary. Bathing suits are optional.

908   HOT SPRINGS RESORT

■   315 Bridge St.   828 622-7676
       Hot Springs, NC 28743
       www.hotspringsspa-nc.com

Picturesque pools and campground on the banks of the French Broad River in the Great Smokey Mountains. The Appalachian Trail runs between the camp sites and the pools. Elevation 2,000 feet. Open all year.

Natural mineral water flows out of a spring at 103° and is piped to twelve secluded, outdoor soaking pools scattered through a wooded area along the river. Pools are cleaned, drained and refilled after each use, so no chemical treatment is required. Some of the pools are covered with an awning for winter use. One pool is handicap accessible. Bathing suits are officially required, but some of the pools are very secluded.

Facilities include 150 camping sites ranging from fifty primitive, shaded sites along the river, fifty with water and electric, and fifty full RV hookups. Group sites can be arranged. There are nine camping cabins and one log cottage with a private mineral water soaking tub. A camping supply and grocery store and a snack bar is on the premises. Massage is also available. A day spa and alternative health center are now open. All other services are one-quarter of a mile away in the town. Credit cards accepted.

Phone for rates, reservations, and directions.

Hot Springs Resort takes very good care of its clientele, providing awnings over several of their pools to keep out the rain, and lattice work around the creekside tubs to provide privacy while soaking.

Photos by Rachel Margolin

The only mineral bathhouse operating in Tennessee offers a warm country setting complete with rocking chairs on the front porch. The twin tubs in the bathhouse are just perfect for a couple to indulge in a little extra romance.

come take the waters.

Ponce de Leon's fabled "Fountain of Youth"

909   THE ARMOUR'S RED BOILING SPRINGS HOTEL

321 E. Main St.   615 699-2180
■ Red Boiling Springs, TN 37150
www.armourshotel.com

Originally built in 1924, this hotel now operates as a bed and breakfast with old-fashioned country atmosphere and a small bathhouse offering private soaks. Open all year.

Mineral water is heated to a comfortable temperature in the two private bathtubs in a separate bathhouse. A one hour treatment consisting of a soak, steam, and massage is offered. Bathing suits not required in the bathhouse.

The twenty beautifully decorated rooms all have private baths and air conditioning. A restaurant is on the premises serving family style meals and all other services are right in the town of Red Boiling Springs. Space is also available for weddings, parties, and reunions. Credit cards accepted. Phone for rates, reservations, and directions.

910   THE SPRINGS—WARM MINERAL HEALING WATERS

12200 San Servando Ave.   941-426-1692
■ Northport, FL 34287
www.warmmineralsprings.com

Spa, health studio, and nearby apartment complex with a nine-million-gallons-per-day mineral spring, located halfway between Fort Meyers and Sarasota. Elevation 10 feet. Open all year.

Mineral water flows out of the ground at 87° and into a two-acre private lake. The lake, which is used for swimming, does not need chlorination because of the volume of flow-through mineral water. The indoor soaking tubs and sauna are under renovation. Call guest services (941 429-0579) for status of construction.

Facilities include a gift shop, bakery and snack bar. Massage, and hot packs are available on the premises. Apartment rentals are nearby. No credit cards accepted. Phone for rates, reservations, and directions.

Safety Harbor Resort and Spa: A retreat for mind, body and soul, offering natural mineral springs spa treatments with more than twenty nutritional, fitness and wellness classes offered daily.

911   SAFETY HARBOR RESORT AND SPA

■   105 N. Bayshore Dr.   888 237-8772
Safety Harbor, FL 34695
www.safetyharborspa.com

An upscale, historic spa, specializing in fitness, beauty and wellness programs, located at the west end of Tampa Bay. Elevation 10 feet. Open all year.

Natural mineral water flows from four springs at approximately 55° and is piped to several pools and to separate men's and women's locker rooms. Gas is used to heat the water. The six individual hydro-tubs in the men's and women's bathhouses are drained and filled after each use so that no chemical treatment of the water is necessary. All other pools are treated with a reverse osmosis procedure requiring very little chlorine treatment. The recreational swimming pool, the lap pool, the indoor exercise pool and the women's plunge pool are maintained at 85°. Two coed hydrojet pools are maintained at 99° and 101°. Handicap accessible. Bathing suits not required in the hydrotubs or plunge pool.

The natural mineral water is also offered throughout the spa and restaurant and used in spa treatments.

Facilities feature a 50,000 square foot spa and fitness facility, with men's and women's locker rooms, showers, sauna, steam room, weight training room, cardio room, two aerobic gyms, and twenty treatment rooms. More than sixty spa and salon treatments and over twenty supervised exercise classes are offered daily. The Phil Green Tennis Academy offers nine courts, while the Golf Academy features a practice range, pro shop and individual instruction. The resort features the Cafe restauranat and Tiki Bar. Credit cards accepted.

Phone for rates, reservations, and directions or visit their web site.

Courtesy of Safety Harbor

Hernando De Soto may or may not have been the first European on the scene, but today's Hot Springs National Park and the surrounding community have their roots in the 1803 Louisiana Purchase. In 1832, Congress took the unprecedented step of establishing public ownership by setting aside four sections of land as a reservation. Unfortunately, no one adequately identified the exact boundaries of this reservation, so the mid-19th century was filled with conflicting claims and counterclaims to the springs and surrounding land.

By 1870, a system evolved that reserved the springs for the Federal Government and sold the developed land to the persons who had settled it. Individual bathhouses on the row collected their own water until 1931 when the 300,000 gallon collection reservoir was built. By 1877, almost all primitive soaking "pits" along Hot Springs Creek were eliminated when the creek was confined to a concrete channel, roofed over, and then paved to create what is now Central Avenue. The "corn hole," used to soak your feet persisted until the early 1990s.

In 1921, The Federal Reservation became Hot Springs National Park, custodian of all the springs and the exclusive contractual supplier of hot mineral water to those elaborate establishments that had become the famous Bathhouse Row. It is also the authority that approves every establishment's rates, equipment, personnel and services related to that water.

In 1949, the Park Service installed air-cooled radiators and tap-water cooled heat exchangers to supply a new central "cool" mineral water reservoir. Now all thermal water customers receive their supply through two pipes, "hot" at 143° and "'cool" at 90°.

During the last four decades, declining patronage forced the closure of many of those historic temples built for "taking the waters." However, the last several years has seen a large resurgence of interest in thermal soaking both for therapy and for pure relaxation, so many of the historic Bathhouse Row locations are being maintained and the NPS hopes to lease them out.

For additional information contact the Hot Springs National Park, PO Box 1860, Hot Springs, AR 71902, 501 624-3383.

912A   BUCKSTAFF BATHS
501 Central Ave.   501 623-2308
Hot Springs, AR 71901

One of the historic Bathhouse Row establishments in continuous operation since 1912, located at the south end of the Row near the Visitor Center. Open all year

Separate men's and women's sections offer one-person soaking tubs that are individually temperature-controlled. They are drained and refilled after each use so no chemical treatment of the water is needed. Along with the bath you also get a sitz bath, hot packs, the use of a vapor/steam cabinet, and a needle shower massage. Whirlpool baths and body massage are available.

Facilities include a third-floor coed lounge with separate men's and women's sun decks at each end. Credit cards accepted.

Courtesy of Hot Springs National Park

In response to the increased interest in stress reduction this family is enjoying a relaxing time together. *Libbey Memorial* is one of the only concessioners actually located in Hot Springs National Park.

912B   LIBBEY MEMORIAL PHYSICAL
        MEDICINE CENTER   501 321-1997
        AND HOT SPRINGS HEALTH SPA

MEDICINE CENTER

Downstairs, a modern, "Medicare-approved, federally regulated" therapy facility and, upstairs, a modern spa with coed soaking tubs, located on Reserve Avenue, three blocks east of Central Avenue. Open all year.

The Libbey Memorial coed thermal whirlpool (105°) and coed exercise pool (98°) are drained and refilled each day, so no chemical treatment of the water is necessary. Facilities include steam and vapor cabinets and electric hoists at therapy pools. Hot packs, massage, and prescribed treatments such as manual therapy, Ultra Sound Therapy, and Electric Stimulation are also available. Credit cards accepted.

HOT SPRINGS HEALTH SPA

    501 Spring St.   501 321-9664
    Hot Springs, AR 71901

The health spa's eight large coed soaking tubs are individually temperature-controlled as desired between 102° and 108°. All are drained and filled each day so that no chemical treatment of the water is necessary. Children are welcome. Massage, steam and vapor cabinets, and exercise equipment are available. Credit cards accepted.

Courtesy of Hot Springs National Park

Catering to therapy needs downstairs and recreational fun upstairs, *Libbey Memorial* appeals to the total hot mineral water marketplace.

Courtesy of Arlington Resort

Water from these springs has been keeping people warm since 1875, when the original Arlington Hotel was opened. The present *Arlington Resort* opened with a gala New Year's Eve party in 1924. Guests from around the world continue to visit this grand Southern Hotel.

912C ARLINGTON RESORT HOTEL & SPA

800 643-1502
In Arkansas 501 623-7771
www.arlingtonhotel.com

A magnificent, luxurious resort in a dominant location overlooking the downtown historic district and Bathhouse Row in Hot Springs National Park.

The in-hotel bathhouse with separate men's and women's sections is open to hotel guests and the public. Private soaking tubs for your mineral water whirlpool bath are individually temperature-controlled and drained after each use so that no chemical treatment of the water is necessary. Massage, hot packs, saunas, sitz-baths, steam baths, and needle showers are available.

A mineral-water hot tub, two tap water swimming pools treated with chlorine, and a multi-level sundeck are reserved for registered guests. The hot tub is maintained at 104°, and the twin pools are maintained at 86° year round.

Facilities include three restaurants and two lounges, beauty and facial salon, exercise room, ballroom, conference and exhibit centers, and shopping mall. All major credit cards accepted.

912D DOWNTOWNER HOTEL & SPA

800 251-1962
501 624-5521

A modern hotel with a large second-floor bathhouse, located on Central Avenue, one block north of Bathhouse Row.

A bathhouse with separate men's and women's sections is open to the public. One-person soaking tubs are individually temperature-controlled and drained after each use so that no chemical treatment of the water is necessary. Whirlpool baths, vapor treatments, hot packs, sitz baths, and massage are available. An outdoor swimming pool and a hot tub are filled with chlorine-treated tap water, and are reserved for the use of registered guests.

Facilities include a beauty salon, sun decks, and a restaurant. Credit cards accepted.

Phil Wilcox

912E HOT SPRINGS HILTON

800 HILTONS
■ ### In Arkansas 501 623-6600

Large, modern resort hotel located next to the Hot Springs Convention Center, two blocks south of Bathhouse Row.

A bathhouse with separate men's and women's sections is open to the public. One-person soaking tubs are individually temperature-controlled and drained after each use so that no chemical treatment of the water is necessary. Massage is available.

An indoor whirlpool (108°) and an indoor-outdoor swimming pool filled with chlorine-treated tap water are reserved for the use of registered guests.

Facilities include restaurants, lounge, meeting rooms and banquet facilities. Major credit cards accepted.

Courtesy of Majestic Resor

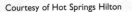
Courtesy of Hot Springs Hilton

912F MAJESTIC HOTEL RESORT SPA

800 643-1504
■ ### In Arkansas 501 623-5511
www.themajestichotel.com

A full-service hotel with bathhouse located in Ho Springs National Park, The Majestic Resort Spa is situate at the north end of Central Avenue.

The best of the the "Old World and New," Traditiona bath house hydrotherapy with thermal mineral wate whirlpool bathing is offered. Separate men's and women individual soaking tubs are temperature-controlled an drained after each use so that no chemical treatment o the water is necessary. Hot packs and Massage are avail able. Full-service Eurpoean-style Body Care Spa and Salo offers: Swedish massages, soothing stone massage Austrian moor body wraps and facials, thalassotherap baths, seaweed mask and wraps, aromatherapy, slat an sugar glows, yoga, chi kung, facials, hair styling, washing manicures and pedicures.

An outdoor swimming pool filled with chlorine-treat ed tap water and heated in the winter is reserved for th use of registered guests.

Facilities include deluxe rooms and suites, two restau rants and a lounge, an old fashioned soda fountain, gift an clothing shops, and conference and banquet rooms. Majo credit cards accepted.

The health spa exterior has been totally renovated to reflect its original art deco theme when it was built in 1936. The lobby still has the original marble floors and columns. The building also serves as the city hall.

I3A HALL OF WATERS SPA AND WATER BAR

201 E. Broadway   816 630-0753
         888 811-0753
Excelsior Springs, MO 64024
www.hallofwaters.com

Originally housing a variety of health-oriented activities and the world's longest mineral water drinking bar, his "Haven of Health" has been completely renovated and is now operated by a private corporation. Elevation 900 feet. Open all year; spa reservations required.

Cold (54°) natural mineral water is pumped from wells (which used to be flowing springs) and is piped to the spa where it is gas-heated and used in individual, private-space tubs. After each use, tubs are drained and refilled so that no chemical treatment of the water is necessary. The bathhouse is coed. The indoor swimming pool, using gas-heated, chlorine-treated tap water, is maintained at approximately 75° and open only in the summer. . A therapeutic pool with a wheelchair ramp is handicap accessible. Bathing suits required..

Facilities include dressing rooms, spa services offering steam and light vapor baths, Scotch needle douche, mud baths, salt glow, body shampoos, toning treatments, raindrop therapy, aromatherpay, and professional therapeutic massage.

The water bar serves as the local Visitors Information Center and headquarters for festivals and special events. Completely restored, you may again sample the original Iron Manganese and Calcium mineral waters that made Excelsior Springs famous. The calcium water is also bottled and sold. The bar sells bottled mineral and flavored waters from around the world. All other services are available close by or in the town. Major credit cards accepted. Phone for rates, reservations, and directions.

Excelsior Springs, called the 'Valley of Vitality" by the Indians has more than forty-nine wells and springs with more naturally occuring types of mineral water than anywhere else in the world.

913B THE ELMS RESORT HOTEL

Regent and Elms Blvd.   816 630-5500
401 Regent St.   800 843-3567
■ Excelsior Springs, MO 64024
www.elmsrest.com

A completely restored historic resort on sixteen acres of rolling hills provides traditional, ancient and contemporary treatments for relaxation, stress reduction and healthy living. One-half hour northeast of Kansas City. Elevation 900 feet. Open all year.

Cold (54°) natural mineral water is pumped from wells on the property and piped to single soaking tubs in separate men's and women's sections. Customers control tub water temperature by adding hot tap water to the cold mineral water as desired. The tubs are drained and filled after each use so no chemical treatment of the water is necessary.

Chlorine-treated tap water is used in all other pools. The indoor European swimming track is maintained at 75°, the one outdoor hot tub pools are maintained at 100°, and the outdoor swimming pool is solar heated. Bathing suits are required in the public-area coed pools. The Spa is open to the public on a limited basis, as well as to registered guests.

The 10,000-foot spa includes cosmetology, hair salon, facials, aloe treatments, herbal wraps, two Swiss and two Vichy showers (in conjunction with other treatments), mineral water and mud bath, sauna and steam rooms, and massage. Classes are offered in yoga and meditation.

Other facilities include 150 individually configured rooms, suites, full conference facilities, two restaurants, a cafe (spa cuisine), fitness center, jogging trails, and tennis courts. A golf course is available. Bicycles are for rent to travel the naturally wooded areas at the resort. A group challenge-course is on the premises. Major credit cards accepted. Phone for rates, reservations, and directions.

914 THE ORIGINAL SPRINGS HOTEL AND BATH HOUSE

618 243-5458
■ Okawville, IL 62271
www.okawvillehotel.com

An authentic 1860s mineral spring resort hotel, located in a small town on I-64, forty-one miles east of St. Louis. Elevation 600 feet. Open all year. Day use customers are welcome.

Natural mineral water flows out of a spring at approximately 50° and is piped to separate men's and women's bathhouses, where it is gas-heated as needed in one-person soaking tubs. Tubs are drained and filled after each use so no chemical treatment of the water is necessary. The indoor/outdoor swimming pool uses gas-heated tap water treated with chlorine, and is maintained at 85°. Bathing suits are not required in bathhouses.

Facilities include historically appointed guest rooms and a restaurant. Spa services including massage and aromatherapy are available on the premises. Credit cards accepted. It is less than four blocks to a service station, store and other services. Phone for rates, reservations, and directions.

915   CLEARWATER HOT TUBS
1201 Butterfield Rd.   630 852-7676
Downers Grove, IL 60515

An upscale rent-a-tub facility located in a suburban town twenty-five miles west of Chicago.

Three different types of suites are available. The spa suite included a tub, shower, dressing area, mood lighting, and music. The VIP suite offers a teak tub, shower over the cub for cool-down, cedar sauna and loft area, mood lighting and music. The party suite's tub has special massage ets and includes the shower, sauna, loft area, a full bath, TV and stereo, mood lighting, and a small fridge with complementary water. Pool temperatures are maintained at approximately 100° in the summer and 104° in the winter. Clothing is optional in the private spaces and required elsewhere.

Massage with steam room is available by appointment. Credit cards accepted. Phone for rates, reservations, and directions.

916   FRENCH LICK SPRINGS RESORT
812 936-9300
■   **French Lick, IN 47432**

The "largest most complete resort in the Midwest," located on 2,600 wooded acres in southwest Indiana, two hours from Indianapolis. Elevation 600 feet. Open all year.

Natural mineral water flows from a spring at 50° and is piped to separate men's and women's bathhouses where it is heated by gas-generated steam, as needed, for one-person soaking tubs. Tubs are drained and filled after each use so no chemical treatment of the water is necessary. All other pools use steam-heated tap water treated with chlorine. The outdoor and indoor whirlpools are maintained at 104°, the dome pool ranges from 72° in the summer to 82° in the winter, and the Olympic swimming pool, for summer use only, is not heated. Bathing suits are required except in bathhouses.

Facilities include two eighteen-hole golf courses, indoor and outdoor tennis courts, equestrian stables and riding trails, guest rooms, nine restaurants and lounges, bowling alleys, conference center, exercise facility, and beauty salon. Massage, body treatments, saunas, steambaths, reflexology, salt rubs, facials, and manicures are available on the premises. Visa, MasterCard, and American Express are accepted. It is three blocks to a service station, store, and other services.

Phone for rates, reservations, and directions.

PUERTO RICO

Information and photos provided by Oscar Voss

The large waist-to-chest deep thermal pool at Banos de Coamo Resort. The temperature in this pool was 102°.

I visited a pair of hot springs south of Coamo, in south central Puerto Rico, a few miles north of the toll road between San Juan and Ponce. The springs, according to legend were the "fountain of youth" that Juan Ponce de Leon was looking for, but missed.

One of the springs supplies a large thermal pool within the parador (country inn), Banos de Coamo Resort, that is open to both overnight guest of the resort, and for a nominal fee ($5 when I visited) to day visitors, from mid-morning to late afternoon. The other spring, which is open to the public at no charge, feeds the pool that is just outside the resort, and is open twenty-four hours a day. A sign posted at the public pools says that swim suits are required and that no pets, food, or alcoholic beverages are allowed.

Directions: From San Juan, take toll route 52 south toward Ponce. Soon after the junction with toll route 53 to Guayama, take exit (salida) 76 looking for route 153 to Santa Isabel and Coamo. This exit comes up with little advance warning, so you need to watch for it. Go 3.3 miles north on route 153, then turn left on route 546. Continue 0.9 miles, past a golf course on the left, to the end of the road where you will find the resort's parking lot, as well as roadside parking just outside the resort if you are only going to the free public spring.

To get to the free spring, instead of turning left into the resort at the end of route 546, walk straight ahead past a gate onto a well-worn dirt path along the resort's perimeter. Walk about 100 yards, and you're there.

GPS: N 18 02.245 W 66 22.438 (resort)
GPS: N 18 02.214 W 66 22.425 (public spring)

The public pools are above this retaining wall, via the ramp ascending to the right. The outflow pipe comes in handy for those who might need to rinse off first before using the pools.

The main pool is waist-deep and is about the same temperature as the source spring—about 108°. There are steps in the pool at the far end, but no other seating, so people either stand or sit on the bottom. The wading pool that you see below the main pool allows parents to easily watch over the children. This pool runs about 100° and is only knee-deep, at most.

A QUICK GPS LESSON

By Chris Andrews

The Global Positioning System (GPS) is a satellite-based navigation system operated by the US Government. It works in any weather conditions, anywhere in the world, 24 hours a day. GPS receivers can provide an electronic 'address' o anything, including hot springs. This address or position is generally expressed in latitude and longitude and accurate within a few dozen yards. There are several different formats used to express the latitude and longitude and converting between them is just simple math. We are using the degrees and minutes (dd mm.mmm) format because it is compatible with most maps and GPS receivers. A minute is just a way to break down a degree. 60 minutes equals one degree. Let's look at a sample position:

N 43 34.680 W 113 09.824

N	designates north of the equator
43	degrees north of the equator
34.680	minutes north of the equator
W	designates west of the Prime Meridian
113	degrees west of the Prime Meridian
09.824	minutes west of the Prime Meridian

To convert a coordinate from the degrees format (dd.dddd) to the degrees and minutes format (dd mm.mmm) jus leave the degrees number the same (43) and take the remaining numbers (.5780) and multiply them times 60 (.5780 × 60 = 34.680)

N 43.5780 = N 43 34.680

To convert a coordinate from the degrees and minutes (dd mm.mmm) format to the degrees format (dd.dddd) jus leave the degrees number the same (43) and take the minutes (34.680) and divide them by 60 (34.680 / 60 = .5780)

N 43 34.680 = N 43.578

Repeat the same process for the longitude number.

So what does it mean to you? Simply enter a hot spring's coordinates from this book into your GPS receiver using the appropriate format. Hit the 'goto' button (or equivalent) and your GPS receiver will point toward the hot spring tell you how far away it is, and what time you will arrive. Press a few more buttons and you will find out what time the sun will set at the hot spring, a very important piece of information when deciding how much beer to pack in and out

GOING NATURAL—PLACES TO STAY

To help those of you who like to stay in places that cater to the naturist lifestyle, included is a list of clubs offering varying types of accommodations. Always call first to check on availability and amenities, and club rules.

CANADA

Alberta

Sunny Chinooks Association
PO Box 33030, 3919 Richmond Road, SW
Calgary, AB T3E 7E2
403 274-8166

British Columbia

Sunny Trails Club
43955 Lougheed Hwy, Box 18
Lake Errock, BC V0M 1N0
604 826-3419

Vancouver Sunbathing Assoc.
10185 164th St.
Surrey, BC V4N 2K4

Van Tan Club
PO Box 423, Stn. A
Vancouver, BC V6C 2N2
604 980-2400

Saskatchewan

Green Haven Sun Club
PO Box 3374
Regina, SK S4P 3H1
306 699-2515

UNITED STATES

Washington

Fraternity Snoqualmie
PO Box 748
Issaquah, WA 98027
425 392-NUDE

Kaniksu Ranch
4295 N. Deer Lake Rd. #5
Loon Lake, WA 99148
509 233-8202

Lake Associates
21700 State Rt. 9
Mt. Vernon, WA 98274
360 445-6833

Lake Bronson Club
PO Box 1135
Sultan, WA 98294
360 793-0286

Oregon

Restful Haven
PO Box 248
North Plains, OR 97133
503 647-2449

Squaw Mountain Ranch
PO Box 4452
Portland, OR 97208
503 630-6136

The Willamettans
PO Box 969
Marcola, OR 97454
541 933-2809

Idaho

BareBackers
PO Box 5781
Boise, ID 83705
208 322-6853

Central, Eastern, Southern States

Central

Blue Lake Club
PO Box 13
Erie, IL 61250
309 659-9297

Fern Hills Club
7330 S. Rockport Rd.
Bloomington, IN 47403
812 824-4489

Lake O'the Woods Club
PO Box 53
Valparaiso, IN 46384

Sunny Haven
11425 Anderson Rd.
Granger, IN 46530
219 277-5356

Sunshower Country Club
PO Box 215
Centerville, IN 47330
765 855-2785

Show-Me Acres
5492 Beach Elk Lane
Stover, MO
573 377-4348

Oaklake Trails
PO Box 470564
Tulsa, OK 74147

Sun Meadow
PO Box 521068
Tulsa, OK 74152
918 266-7651

Eastern

Berkshire Vista Resort
312 Kittle Rd.
Hancock, MA 01237
413 738-5154

Sandy Terraces
PO Box 98
Marstons Mills, MA 02648
508 428-9209

Buckridge Nudist Park
21 S. Tuttle Hill Rd.
Candor, NY 13743
607 659-3868

Empire Haven
5947 Sun Lane
Moravia, NY 13118
315 497-0135

Southern

Caliente Resort
6500 Land O'Lakes Blvd.
Land O'Lakes, FL 34639
813 996-3700

Club Paradise
PO Box 750
Land O'Lakes, FL 34639
800 237-2226

Cypress Cove
4425 Pleasant Hill Rd.
Kissimmee, FL 34746
407 933-5870

Gulf Coast Resort
13220 Houston Ave.
Hudson, FL 34667-6101
813 868-1061

The Island Group
22146 Dupree Dr.
Land O'Lakes, FL 34639

Lake Como Club
20500 Cot Rd.
Lutz, FL 33549

Riviera Naturist Resort
PO Box 2233
Pace, FL 32572
850 994-3665

Seminole Health Club
3800 SW 142nd Ave.
Davie, FL 33330
954 473-0231

Sunburst Resort
2375 Horn Rd.
Milton, FL 32570
904 675-6807

Sunny Sands Resort
502 Central Blvd.
Pierson, FL 32180-2323
904 749-2233

Sunsport Gardens
14125 North Rd.
Loxahatchee, FL 33470
561 793-0423

Bar-S-Ranch
313 Bar-S-Trail
Reidsville, NC 27320
910 349-2456

Nirvana Sun Resort
65 Harbour Dr.
Tabor City, NC 28463
800 378-7072

Whispering Pines
1114 Sun St. Shallotte,
NC 28459

Rock Haven Lodge
462 Rock Haven Rd.
Murfreesboro, TN 37127
615 896-3553

Timberline Lodge Resort
500 Timerbline Ln.
Crossville, TN 38555
800 TAN-NUDE

White Tail Park
39033 White Tail Drive
Ivor, VA 23866
800 987-6833

Avalon
PO Box 369
PawPaw, WV 25434
304 947-5600

INDEX

This index is designed to help you locate a listing when you start with the location name. The description of the location will be found on the page number given for that name.

Within the index the abbreviations listed below are used to identify the specific state or geographical area of the location. The number shown after each state listed below is the page number where the **KEY MAP** of that state will be found.

AK=ALASKA / 14
CD=CANADA / 26
ID=IDAHO / 90
MT=MONTANA / 162
OR=OREGON / 64
WA=WASHINGTON / 52
WY=WYOMING / S. DAKOTA / 178
ST=CENTRAL, EASTERN, SOUTHERN / 196

NUBP=NOT USABLE BY THE PUBLIC

S

SACAJAWEA HOT SPRINGS ID 143
SAFETY HARBOR RESORT & SPA ST 204
SALMON HOT SPRING ID 102
SAND SPRINGS POOL ST 197
SARATOGA INN RESORT WY 182
SAWTOOTH LODGE ID 143
SCENIC HOT SPRINGS WA 55
SERPENTINE HOT SPRINGS AK 16
SHARKEY HOT SPRING ID 102
SHEEP CREEK BRIDGE HOT SPRINGS
                        ID 141
SHOWER BATH HOT SPRINGS ID 101
SILVER CREEK PLUNGE ID 150
SKILLERN HOT SPRINGS ID 130
SKINNY DIPPER HOT SPRINGS ID 147
SKOOKUMCHUCK HOT SPRINGS CD 35
SLATE CREEK HOT SPRING ID 123
SLIGAR'S THOUSAND SPRINGS RESORT
                        ID 117
SLOQUET CREEK HOT SPRINGS CD 36
SMITH CABIN HOT SPRINGS ID 141
SNIVELY HOT SPRINGS OR 69
SOL DUC HOT SPRINGS WA 62
SOUTH HARNEY LAKE HOT SPRINGS OR 76
THE SPA ST 197
SPA HOT SPRING MOTEL MT 165
SPRINGFIELD SPAS OR 82
SPRINGS BATH HOUSE WY/SD 195
THE SPRINGS WARM MINERAL HEALING
            WATERS ST 203
ST. LEON HOT SPRINGS CD 40
ST. MARTINS ON THE WIND WA 57
STANLEY HOT SPRING ID 91
STAR PLUNGE WY 181
STATE BATH HOUSE WY 180
SUGAH (MILE 16) HOT SPRING ID 155
SUMMER LAKE HOT SPRINGS OR 76
SUNBEAM HOT SPRINGS ID 123
SUNFLOWER FLATS HOT SPRINGS ID 98
SYMES HOT SPRINGS HOTEL AND
            MINERAL BATHS MT 175

T

TAKHINI HOT SPRINGS AK 28
TEMPLE GARDENS MINERAL SPA CD 51
TENAKEE HOT SPRINGS AK 21
TEPEE SPA WY 180
TERWILIGER (COUGAR) HOT
            SPRINGS OR 81
THREE FORKS HOT SPRINGS OR 71

TOLO VISTA MOTEL WA 55
TOLOVANA HOT SPRINGS AK 18
TRAIL CREEK HOT SPRING ID 153
TUBS SEATTLE WA 60
TUMBLING WATERS MOTEL ID 110
TWIN SPRINGS ID 142

U

UMPQUA WARM SPRING OR 78
UPPER LOON CREEK HOT SPRING ID 125
UPTOWN VILLAGE HEALTH CENTER WA 58

V

VULCAN HOT SPRINGS ID 155

W

WALL CREEK WARM SPRING see
            MEDITATION POOL OR 80
WARFIELD HOT SPRING ID 129
WARM SPRINGS CREEK ID 105
WEIR CREEK HOT SPRINGS ID 92
WELLSPRING WA 59
WEST PASS HOT SPRING ID 122
WHITE LICKS HOT SPRINGS ID 157
WHITEHORSE RANCH HOT SPRING OR 72
WHITE SULPHER HOT SPRINGS AK 22
WHITEY COX HOT SPRINGS ID 98
WILD HORSE HOT SPRINGS MT 177
WILD ROSE HOT SPRINGS ID 119
WILLOW CREEK HOT SPRINGS ID 132
WORSWICK HOT SPRINGS ID 129

Z

ZIM'S HOT SPRINGS ID 159

Every edition we loose a few hot springs to natural causes such as fire or flood. Sometimes springs are lost to us
by people's refusal to take care of them and the subse-
quent destruction by an official governmen agency. And,
sometimes, the causes are unclear. Here's to those we
lost this edition:

    The Alaskan Hotel
    Scenic Hot Springs (dead, but not buried)
    Hunter's Hot Springs Resort
    Warm Springs Resort
    Deer Creek Hot Springs
    Waterhole Lodge
    Krigbaum Hot Springs
    Astoria Mineral Hot Springs
    Madison Campground
    Cottonwood Hot Springs Spa

I am happy to report, however, that we added many more
springs to the book than we lost!

One of the best set of signs I have seen in all my
hot springs travels! Posted outside the town of
Bruneau, Idaho on the way to and from Lower
Indian Bathtub Hot Springs.

HOT Springs
& Hot Pools
of the Northwest

ALASKA	CANADA
IDAHO	WYOMING/S.DAKOTA
OREGON	WASHINGTON
MONTANA	
CENTRAL, EASTERN, SOUTHERN	
STATES	

$19.95 ISBN 1-890880-04-3

HOT Springs
& Hot Pools
of the Southwest

CALIFORNIA	UTAH
ARIZONA	COLORADO
NEW MEXICO	NEVADA
TEXAS	BAJA (MEXICO)

$19.95 ISBN 1-890880-03-5

Jayson Loam's original best-selling regional guides to places where you can go and legally put your body in hot water. Edited and produced by Marjorie Gersh-Young.

Our easy-to-use format provides a complete description and a specific key map location for every spring listed.

Dozens of maps and hundreds of photos help you make an informed choice, tell you how to get there, and show you what to expect when you arrive. GPS coordinates included.

Descriptions of primitive free-flowing hot springs and commercial springs include description of physical surroundings, bathing suit customs, directions, and distances to a campground and other services.

These guides also include drilled hot wells and private gas-heated tap water pools for rent by the hour.

Name			
Street			
City		State	Zip
		Order Quan.	Amount
Hot Springs and Hot Pools of the Northwest $19.95			
Hot Springs and Hot Pools of the Southwest $19.95			
Postage: $3 first book, $2 each additional book			
Canadians: Please send in US dollars			
BOOK Make check to: AQUA THERMAL ACCESS 831 426-2956 **MAIL ORDER** Mail to: 55 Azalea Lane, Santa Cruz, CA 95060			TOTAL

The **Hot Springs** *Gazette*

A Dippers' Guide to Hot
Springs Throughout the
West and Elsewhere

Each issue highlights one or two areas of natural hot springs, complete with great stories and anecdotes.

Also includes updates, information on books and maps, the Internet, and bits of this and that.

Edited by Skip Hill

Published Quarterly
Single copy price: US $5.00, plus $1.00 postage
Subscription rate per year: US $20.00

Check the Gazette out at: http://www.hotspringsgazette.com

If you discover something at a hot springs that needs to be revised,
or you come across additional information that you would like to pass along, write, phone, fax, or email
to:
Aqua Thermal Access
55 Azalea Lane
Santa Cruz, CA 95060
phone and fax: 831 426-2956
email: hsprings@ix.netcom.com

May You Soak in Peace!